Today, our society is facing a new mental health crisis . . . an epidemic of loneliness. In *The Path out of Loneliness*, Dr. Mark Mayfield provides readers with a new way to be seen, heard, and loved. A timely must-read!

DR. TIM CLINTON, president of American Association of Christian Counselors, executive director of James Dobson Family Institute

Dr. Mark Mayfield's new book, *The Path out of Loneliness*, skillfully highlights a very urgent problem in our society today: isolation and its physical and mental consequences—and what we can do about it. He delves into the many social aspects of loneliness in a way that is both accessible and understandable, providing the reader with the knowledge and resources to combat this far-reaching issue.

DR. CAROLINE LEAF, cognitive neuroscientist, mental health expert, bestselling author

Loneliness is a risk factor for Alzheimer's disease and many psychiatric problems. We MUST address this issue head on, or the current mental health pandemic will continue to spiral out of control. Dr. Mark Mayfield's new book, *The Path out of Loneliness*, does this in an elegant way. I highly recommend it.

DANIEL G. AMEN, MD, founder of Amen Clinics, author of *Your Brain Is Always Listening*

For the price of this book, you get a year's worth of counseling . . . at your own pace. From a smart and compassionate therapist!

JOHN ELDREDGE, *New York Times* bestselling author, counselor

We were made for community. Yet our brokenness often makes us hide from others and keeps us from loving people well. As a counselor, as a professor, and as one who has served as a pastor, Mayfield integrates principles and practices from faith and science to help us flourish in fellowship with one another. This book will guide you toward wholeness as you and I learn to give and receive love.

REV. DR. GLENN PACKIAM, associate senior pastor at New Life Church, author of *Blessed Broken Given*

We've got to start seeing deep connection as a requirement, not an accessory in our lives. Dr. Mayfield has written this incredible, holistic guide to help you fight loneliness in your own life and see how God hardwired you for relationships.

>JENNIE ALLEN, *New York Times* bestselling author of *Get Out of Your Head*, founder and visionary of IF:Gathering

Before anyone ever heard of the COVID-19 pandemic, loneliness was already a plague among us, but it was greatly exacerbated by the deadly virus separating us into our socially isolated cocoons. Whatever the cause, loneliness can drag us down into a debilitating spiral of despair, hopelessness, sickness, insanity, even death. There's a reason prisons reserve solitary confinement as one of their harshest punishments.

Loneliness has its genesis in Genesis, which makes clear it is not what God intended for us. We were lovingly created for relationship and connection—with him and with others. Within these pages, walk step-by step with Mark as he gently guides you out of the darkness, offering practical tools such as honesty, vulnerability, reflection, and awareness, and let the insights gleaned lead you to embrace hope as you discover your identity, meaning, and purpose on the other side of loneliness.

>DR. WESS STAFFORD, president emeritus of Compassion International, author of *Too Small to Ignore* and *Just a Minute*

Power-packed with his own vulnerable stories and strengthened through living examples curated from thousands of counseling clients, Dr. Mayfield guides us through today's pressing problems, recovers original design, and gently and courageously guides us on a path toward hope.

>MORGAN SNYDER, author of *Becoming a King*, vice president of Wild at Heart, founder of BecomeGoodSoil.com

I've seen Mark Mayfield at work as a counselor, and now I know him as a friend. I've witnessed firsthand his passion for soul health, and I've watched him nurture a city toward life. *The Path out of Loneliness* is a clear call for us to get back to what we were made for—connection. This is a lifesaving message. Thank you, Mark, for being a voice.

>JON EGAN, music artist, worship pastor at New Life Church

THE PATH

FINDING AND FOSTERING

OUT OF

CONNECTION TO GOD, OURSELVES,

LONELINESS

AND ONE ANOTHER

DR. MARK MAYFIELD

Foreword by Curt Thompson, MD

A NavPress resource published in alliance
with Tyndale House Publishers

NavPress is the publishing ministry of The Navigators, an international Christian organization and leader in personal spiritual development. NavPress is committed to helping people grow spiritually and enjoy lives of meaning and hope through personal and group resources that are biblically rooted, culturally relevant, and highly practical.

For more information, visit NavPress.com.

To my wife and best friend, Sarah. Thank you for partnering with me on this wild adventure called life. I love you!

CONTENTS

Foreword

IN 2018, the United Kingdom appointed its first Minister for Loneliness. By then we had begun to recognize that for all of our modern advances, we were—and are—still as alienated as Cain was from Abel. Often, by the time a public health concern reaches the halls of government, one knows that it has long since perniciously been active and debilitating in the community. And so, as I write this at the commencement of 2021, in the case of loneliness, despite our scientific specialization, communication, and affluence, we find ourselves overwhelmed not by one but two pandemics—one viral and the other simply human.

Over the past thirty years, as I have treated patients who suffer from various psychiatric maladies, the specter of loneliness has hovered everywhere. And with each patient, it eventually makes its way into the conversation. We are people who are fraught, both neurobiologically and relationally, with a deep and ancient sense of alienation, of being cut off. Cut off from parts of ourselves and from each other. As we read in Scripture's Creation texts, it is not good to be alone. But like our first parents, we continue to blindly—or in some cases, quite consciously—make choices that exacerbate our loneliness, only to find that our states of trauma, anxiety, depression, and addiction worsen, driving those very behaviors that serve only to reinforce the cycle of loneliness we are trying so desperately to escape.

Life on this earth was not meant to be this way. Nor does it have to be. With *The Path out of Loneliness*, Mark Mayfield not only shines a bright light on our topic's features but, throughout the book, he looks to fire the reader's imagination with hope—hope that loneliness is not the final state of affairs that any of us has to live with.

He begins by drawing the reader's attention to the impact of loneliness and the extent to which it reaches into our public domains and into the privacy of our souls. He deftly provides a stark account of where we find ourselves and the complex layers of life that contribute to the problem.

But Mark does not leave us there. For indeed, he is a clinician who knows of what he speaks; he does not live with the illusion that combatting our foe will be easy, nor does he offer a simple checklist of things to do that will somehow magically solve a complex problem. Rather, he does what any thoughtful clinician does: He offers himself—with vulnerability and precision—as a guide who deeply longs for his readers to tell their stories more truly, and so to live into the lives of beauty and goodness that they were destined for from the beginning.

Hence, he immerses us in the biblical narrative, setting us firmly in the context of God's story—one in which, despite the choices we have made over time that lead to painful alienation one from the other, he has no intention of leaving us where we are.

Throughout the book, Mark provides examples of real

experience that capture our emotion while providing accompanying instruction to help us understand what those stories really mean. He winsomely and practically introduces us to the important themes of neuroscience and attachment that so effectively enable us to better understand God's intention for us as humans. He then helps us see how loneliness is ultimately symptomatic of our moving away from God's story as we try to cope with our own, on our own.

Finally—and joyfully—our author paves a beautiful, clear path of application: of the practices that enable us to make the difficult changes that will be necessary on our journey to wholeness. He weaves biblical wisdom with his work as a seasoned and humble mental health care provider to present to us a gift that is born out of the personal work that Mark has done and that is evident on the pages you read. He doesn't ask any of us to do something he has not been willing to do himself.

I know Mark Mayfield to be a man of integrity, a therapist of deep thirst for learning, and a man who is as kind as he is wise. He has the professional experience that anyone would want in their clinician—and he has the humility to know that he offers us his brokenness as much as anything on our road to healing. It is with this awareness of all that Mark hopes for you, the reader, to gain from this book that I commend it to your reading.

Read it with curiosity. Read it prepared to work. But mostly, read it in anticipation that the God of creation is coming to find you in your loneliness in order to transform you and the lives of those you will love as a result.

Curt Thompson, MD
Author of The Soul of Shame *and* Anatomy of the Soul

Introduction

The most terrible poverty is loneliness,
and the feeling of being unloved.
MOTHER TERESA

HAVE YOU EVER SLOWED DOWN, sat back, and watched people? I find it fascinating to observe people in their different environments. Maybe it's the counselor in me, or maybe it's the researcher, but I'm intrigued by body language, facial features and expressions, walk, dress, communication, and so on. Each feature tells a fascinating story if you know what to look for.

I recently traveled to Washington, DC, for a business trip, and during my time in between airports, planes, and taxis, a great deal of my time was spent observing people and their behaviors. I started to notice that almost everyone was looking down. Their shoulders were slumped, their faces were downcast, and their gazes were squarely on their mobile device or screen. I very rarely made eye contact with anyone, but when I did, the other person would

1

quickly look away, almost blushing with embarrassment. It was as if I could hear them thinking, *Oh! You're looking at me, and you see me; I'm not sure what to do with that!* Their eyes would quickly drop back to their device.

Inability to look a stranger in the eye is one thing, but inability to connect in a deep conversation with a friend or family member takes our disengagement to a whole different level. I see this happening everywhere I go. Next time you're at a "sit down" restaurant, take a look around and count how many people have their phones out and are disengaged from those at their table. There is little-to-no conversation and much distraction from being present.

Avoidance leads to disconnectedness. It reminds me of the Disney/Pixar movie *WALL-E*.[1] WALL-E is a garbage robot left on earth to clean up the extreme waste of the human race, who has destroyed the earth and left to find a better place to inhabit. Though I appreciate the "save the earth" messaging, I quickly picked up on the subversive undertones. WALL-E was accidentally taken up to space and deposited on a space shuttle filled with people who ate all the time and were constantly engaged with the latest technology. Thanks to lack of muscle use, they were unable to walk. It was not until WALL-E and EVE (another robot) disrupted the norm that people were able to look up and notice each other.

This movie was an eerie prophetic foreshadowing of what's beginning to happen in our culture. Ironically, *WALL-E* was released one year after the first iPhone came out. Since then, the foundation of our culture has changed. We are the most connected generation in history, yet we are also the loneliest generation. This is exemplified in a 2018 survey that revealed that 17 percent of those surveyed were lonely, while 54 percent struggled with aspects of loneliness.[2]

Laying the blame of all our societal problems on a device is not realistic, but the newest technology certainly is representative of a bigger, more complex problem. As I consider the state of our country and our world, I'm perplexed by the statistics. Why, in a more advanced society, are we dying ten to fifteen years earlier than we were in past generations? Why is the suicide rate continuing to increase in spite of advanced prevention, treatment, and postvention[3] efforts? Why is the addiction crisis still growing despite the hard-fought efforts of nonprofits, treatment centers, and government entities? Why are depression and anxiety on the rise, with no signs of slowing down? Why are heart disease, cardiovascular disease, and cancer worse now than they were a decade ago, despite so many medical "advancements"?

The answer can be both simple and complex. We are relational beings who need eye-to-eye, face-to-face contact and proximity on a regular basis. As a society, we are operating out of significant deficits.

Many of you might be reading this and thinking, *I'm not lonely! I've got a great spouse, a fantastic family, and friends. Why would I be lonely?* But deep down inside, you've experienced that nagging feeling of fear, anxiety, depression, or isolation. You've questioned when the last time you were truly seen as a person, loved for who you are, and valued as a unique human soul. Yes, bouts of loneliness are a common spiritual condition of humans, but prolonged loneliness is a sign of a deeper disconnect. In many ways, as a society, we've lost the ability to connect on a deep, messy, soul-seeing level. We've lost the ability to admit we need help and then ask for it. We're a lonely society, and with loneliness comes isolation, and with isolation comes death—in our mind, body, and spirit.

This doesn't have to be the way life ends. This book is meant to offer hope, to be a catalyst for change that is not based on the latest mental health fad or societal trends. *The Path out of Loneliness* is a real advocate for substantial change to reconnect people and help them be seen again.

The book is broken into three distinct parts. Part I explores the current and historical factors that brought us to this point. Part II engages in a conversation on the way it was originally designed. Part III discusses how to realign our lives so that we can change internally and, as a result, become change agents in our homes, neighborhoods, communities, and places of worship. For this to happen, we need to rethink and reimagine how to combat this loneliness epidemic.

Part I

THE PROBLEM

LONELINESS

The Basic Crisis of a Modern Society

To think that two bodies, crooked by life into question marks, when encountering one another did not form a heart. To do that, all we needed was to look each other in the eye, but you looked away.

ANNA JAE

Because Adam chose the pleasures of sin, humanity has inherited the pain of loneliness and the pain of separation from God and others. At its root, loneliness began in the garden of Eden, and we are all children of Eden.

PAUL MATTHIES, "ONLY THE LONELY"

I LOVE EPIC TRILOGIES. The *Lord of the Rings* trilogy by J. R. R. Tolkien is one of my favorites. (I'm a huge fan of the extended-version director's cut of the Peter Jackson adaptation, just in case there was any question or debate.) They were my favorite book series as a kid growing up, and the movies captured the attention to detail of my imagination. It was almost as if Peter Jackson were in my head as he directed the movies. What makes a trilogy like *The Lord of the Rings* so good? In my opinion, there are several key components:

1. solid, dynamic, and engaging characters;
2. a solid story line;
3. development of a problem that must be solved;

4. an epic struggle between good and evil;
5. a climax to the story that engages every aspect of your humanity (mind, body, spirit); and
6. resolution and redemption.

These components are woven into every minor and macro detail of Tolkien's work. Many other prolific writers have written epic stories similar to Tolkien's, which causes me to pause and wonder, *Why?* What if these stories are just reflections, echoes of a bigger story of good versus evil, of struggle, pain, loneliness, and redemption? What if these stories are the deep longings of our souls? The longings to be seen, to be known, to be loved, and to be valued?

Biblical Origins of Loneliness

The Bible is one of those epic stories, a story of love, loss, pain, sorrow, loneliness, rescue, and redemption. If you've never stopped to pick up a Bible and read through it, I'd encourage you to do so. The Bible tells the story of rescue and redemption that is weaved throughout history. A telling of souls lost and brought back to intentional love.

Loneliness, it turns out, enters the story very early. The creation narrative introduces us to several key characters. God, the protagonist, who existed before all things, effortlessly but intentionally spoke life into existence. As we see in Genesis chapter 1, God created the heavens and the earth, the land and the seas, the birds of the air, the fish of the sea, and the animals of the land. He looked around and saw that what he'd created was good, but something was missing. Relationship. Fellowship. Connection. Though these things were represented in the Trinity, it wasn't yet represented on earth. God created mankind in his image, "male and female he created them" (Genesis 1:27, ESV). I've read this story over and over, and each time, I'm overwhelmed. The God of the universe, of countless stars and galaxies, desired that we share in his creation. From the start, he wanted to be in an intimate, reciprocal relationship with us.

But the perfection of the original design didn't last long. Adam and Eve quickly met the antagonist of the story, Satan, in the form of a serpent. Satan began to plant seeds of doubt into Adam and Eve, causing them to question God's original design. The seed of deceit grew, and both Adam and Eve ate from the fruit from the tree of the knowledge of good and evil. Let's look at Genesis 3:7-10 (NIV), which contains several components that lay the foundation for our current loneliness epidemic:

> Then the eyes of both of them were opened, and they realized they were naked; so they sewed fig leaves together and made coverings for themselves.
>
> Then the man and his wife heard the sound of the LORD God as he was walking in the garden in the cool of the day, and they hid from the LORD God among the trees of the garden. But the LORD God called to the man, "Where are you?"
>
> He answered, "I heard you in the garden, and I was afraid because I was naked; so I hid."

In the Septuagint, the earliest Greek translation of the Hebrew Scriptures, the word used for "eyes" is *ophthalmos*, which refers both to literal and figurative sight. This means that their mind's eye and their awareness of both good and evil was opened. This awareness didn't lead to greater understanding; it led to greater fear and separation. God knew that the human intellect couldn't comprehend the mind of God, so it was his plan to protect them from this amount of knowledge and awareness. Instead, the planted lie of the serpent grew in Adam and Eve, and they thought they knew better. In that moment, separation, fear, anxiety, confusion, shame, and blame established the problem of loneliness. We've been searching for redemption ever since.

The Crisis Continues

"The eyes are the window to the soul." I've heard this phrase my whole life. When was the last time you slowed down and noticed someone? Was it your spouse? A friend? A colleague? A stranger? Think back—do you have that mental picture in your head? Now, focus on their eyes. What story did they tell? Joy? Sorrow? Hope? Despair? Confusion? Contentment? If you didn't hold their gaze long enough to determine this, why? Were you uncomfortable? Scared? Uncertain?

Whatever your reasons, you aren't alone. The average length of a mutual gaze is three seconds.[1] *Three seconds!* Three seconds to determine how someone is doing. Seems impossible, right? Well, in all actuality, it is! There is little-to-no possibility of assessing the health and well-being of someone if we're unwilling or unable to peer into their soul.

Why are the eyes so important? The eyes have a way of telling a story where words often fail. Eyes will tell you if a smile is real or not because eyes will often smile first. Pupil dilatation is a sign of engagement and interest. A mutual gaze is a sign of affection and love. Though the appropriate length of time a person should hold a gaze is debated, eye-to-eye connection is an important tool in the development of relationships and attachment.

Many years before I was a counselor or had a doctorate, I was a youth and family pastor at a small church in the Rocky Mountains of Colorado. As a young, single, recent college graduate, I found this an ideal job—if you could even call it a job. I was paid to hang out with middle school and high school youth, create programs, teach them about the Scriptures, and walk with them along life's journey. To top it off, I lived within fifteen minutes of four of the best ski resorts in the country. Part of the fun was getting to play in the two-hundred-plus inches of snow every year by getting first tracks (the first ski run of the day after a big snow). It was an amazing place to live!

One of my routines each week was to meet with my students at the local main-street coffee shop. I'd set aside around two hours for students to "drop in" for coffee and conversation with their youth pastor. Some weeks, I'd have five to eight students show up; other weeks, I'd have one or two. One week, I had only one show up—a kid named Tre.[2] Tre was one of my ninth-grade students. Born and raised in this mountain town, he was a moderately extroverted young man with a very dry sense of humor, one that was mature beyond his years. He made many adults laugh while causing his peers to scratch their heads. If this wasn't enough to make him stand out, his tall, lanky stature solidified his awkwardness. If you met Tre for the first time, you'd assume everything was okay as he presented himself as having it all together. He played off his awkwardness with a skilled sense of humor that could get a room full of adults laughing within a matter of seconds. But it was all a diversion, a carefully planned defense mechanism to keep people from getting too close.

I got to know Tre over the course of a couple of years and learned that his parents were first-generation entrepreneurs looking to prove themselves and achieve status in this rich mountain town. Tre's dad owned several trendy restaurants in the area, while Tre's mom was a successful realtor. Thus, Tre's parents were rarely home. An only child, Tre was often left by himself to finish his homework, eat dinner, do chores, and put himself to bed. Tre came to every event we put on at the church and was very active in the youth group, but he kept people at a distance.

This was my first one-on-one with Tre, and it was a divine arrangement. Tre walked into the coffee shop, surveyed the room, and quickly realized he was going to be by himself with me. He briefly made eye contact, and I could almost hear his mind screaming, *Great! No one else is here. That means I have to actually talk with Mark.* Before he could escape, I jumped up out of my seat. "Tre!" I exclaimed, "Good to see you today!" I motioned to the counter, "What do you want? I'm buying." I said.

Caught a bit off guard, Tre approached the counter and ordered a large milkshake. I ordered the same. As we returned to our seats, I asked the generic question, "How are you?" He briefly looked at me and then quickly looked down to find his straw. After taking a large sip of his milkshake, he looked up and replied, "Okay," in a forced jovial voice.

Pausing for a second and holding his gaze for a couple more seconds, I could tell something was slightly off today. "Okay?" I responded. "That doesn't sound convincing." I paused and asked, "What's really going on?"

I could tell Tre realized I'd seen right through him. For a moment, he looked trapped. His eyes darted back and forth as he looked for a way to avoid the deeper question. Without any diversion, Tre took a deep breath and proceeded to say, "Mark, I'm . . . I'm . . . so lonely."

As he said those words, he broke down and started to cry right there in the bustling coffee shop. I sat with Tre for several hours that day, allowing him to be truly seen and heard for the first time in his life. He revealed that he'd been fighting loneliness for several months, and while he was not currently suicidal, he had, at times, contemplated suicide. He went on to disclose that he'd begun experimenting with drugs, attempting to numb the pain.

I was honored that Tre shared these things with me, yet it angered me that he'd had to carry this burden by himself for so long. In the days and weeks following our coffee-shop conversation, I was able to support Tre by facilitating a couple of heart-to-heart conversations with his parents. Tre was able to express how he was feeling, and, to my surprise, his parents were able to listen with minimal defensiveness. They came up with a plan where, after school, Tre would join his dad several times a week at the restaurants, and he would join his mom on several of her showings throughout the week. They also agreed to have dinner together three times a week, and both mom and dad agreed to take Sundays off.

This was a great outcome to a potentially volatile situation. I often wonder what would've happened to Tre if he and I hadn't met for coffee that day. Or if I hadn't slowed down to pay attention to the warning signs. Or if I'd accepted his superficial responses. What would have been the outcome? Would he have taken his life? I shudder at the possibility.

My focus then shifts to wondering how many people in my life are currently suffering silently and are unable or unwilling to ask for help. As I look around and observe others in our culture,

I wonder how many people are silently suffering in loneliness and wandering about in despair. *Why do we see asking for help as a sign of weakness instead of a sign of strength?* In my humble opinion, this question is the problem with the basic crisis of our contemporary society.

What Is Loneliness?

What does it mean to be lonely? How do we nail down a comprehensive and universal definition of loneliness? Defining terms can be a laborious process that takes years of research. I want to make this simple, so instead of throwing a wad of statistics and studies at you, I'm just going to give you questions to consider.

First, I want you to ground yourself in this moment, the one right now as you are reading these words on this page. Sit up in your chair and have your feet firmly planted on the ground. (I'm serious—do it! This posture will help you focus.)

Now, when you hear the word *lonely*, what is the first thing that comes to mind? Is it being alone? Isolated? Fearful? Is it loss? Or grief? What is it?

When that word or thought came to your mind, what did you feel in your body? Panic? Anxiety? Depression? Sorrow? Sadness? Where did you feel it in your body? Your head? Chest? Shoulders? Stomach?

When I think about loneliness, I think about relational isolation. I think about being misunderstood, dismissed, unseen, invalidated, or invaluable. When I feel it in my body, I feel it in several places. First, I feel it in my throat, like I have something stuck there and I cannot speak or I have lost my voice. Second, I feel it in the pit of my stomach, almost as if I were riding up a roller coaster, getting ready for it to drop.

Dictionary definitions of *lonely* yield vague descriptions:

- "Being without company."
- "Cut off from others."
- "Not frequented by human beings."
- "Sad from being alone."
- "Producing a feeling of bleakness or desolation."[3]

Such definitions do not paint the depth of the actuality of the feeling or experience. For many of us, our definition of loneliness is born of our experience. I want you to connect with that definition and hold it loosely as you read this book. Your experience is your lens and current reality, and it's valid. I will share my own definition of loneliness at the conclusion of this chapter.

Unique feelings accompany loneliness, and, in my opinion, those feelings are specific to the one experiencing it. To begin to develop a deeper understanding of this topic, I created an online survey for individuals to fill out anonymously. I asked five questions:

1. On a scale of 1 (not lonely) to 5 (very lonely), how lonely do you feel on a daily basis?
2. In your own words, how would you define *loneliness*?
3. When you feel lonely, what do you typically do to feel better?
4. Why do you think loneliness is on the rise in our culture?
5. If you had a magic wand and could fix the loneliness around you, what would you do?

I recognize that there's not much of a scientific framework in this survey, and the answers won't produce a statistical analysis of loneliness, but that's okay. I wanted to understand the lived experiences of the individuals answering the survey. I wanted to hear what was said and observe what was not said. There were 168 participants from 28 US states and 3 additional countries. Here's what I found (see Figure 1).

On a scale of 1 (not lonely) to 5 (very lonely), 26 percent of people surveyed said they weren't lonely (1), 28 percent said they were slightly lonely (2), 28.6 percent said they were moderately lonely (3), and 17.3 percent said they were significantly lonely (4/5). The average overall loneliness score was a 2.4 out of 5.

Loneliness Scale

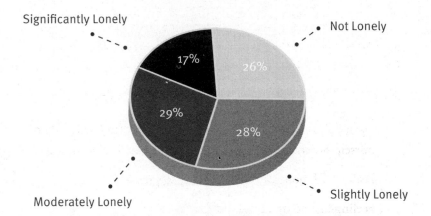

Being a geeky researcher, I wanted to see if other studies out there would correlate to my small survey. Cigna, a major player in the insurance world, did a loneliness survey of twenty thousand adults ages eighteen and older.[4] They found that on a loneliness scale ranging from 20 (less lonely) to 80 (very lonely), the average of all responses was 44, which is very similar to my survey results. They found that:

- 54 percent of people surveyed felt no one knew them well.
- 46 percent reported feeling alone, with 47 percent feeling left out.
- 43 percent lacked companionship.
- 43 percent felt their relationships weren't meaningful.
- 43 percent felt isolated from others.
- 39 percent no longer felt close to anyone.
- 59 percent felt like their interests and ideas weren't shared by others.
- 36 percent didn't feel like they had anyone to turn to.

Though these statistics are interesting, they don't get to the heart of the matter: lived experiences. Circling back to my survey, I want to focus on two of the five questions. I asked participants to define loneliness. Here are some of their answers[5]:

"Feeling despair at times, exhaustion, immobil[ity], keeping to yourself, not knowing how to fix it."

"Feeling sad, hopeless, self-isolation, depression."

"Feeling like no one cares for you."

"The absence of human connection. You can physically have people around you but experience no movement from them toward you."

"Feeling isolated, even when surrounded by people."

"The absence of deeper connection and understanding by others."

"The only sounds you can hear are your own echoes."

"Feeling like you are all alone mentally and emotionally. Even if you are married or surrounded by people, you still feel like no one really knows the real you."

"Not feeling seen, heard, or known."

"No one to share my heart with."

"Loneliness can feel much like depression, though I wonder if it has a sharper edge to it that is personal, as if you have been singled out as being unworthy of companionship, friendship, or love."

There were many more responses that could've been placed here, but these captured the essence and depth of the rest of the 168 participants. I found it interesting that a major theme was *not feeling seen, heard, or understood.* We'll talk more about this in later chapters.

I then asked the question: Why? Why are so many souls in our world struggling with loneliness? Why is this epidemic growing? And why is it moving to a pandemic, with no signs of slowing? Here are some of the answers to that question:

"We are so obsessed with posting and getting likes that we mistake reactions and comments for relationship. We are so unused to conversation that even the thought of talking with a friend can produce anxiety."

"Too much electronic entertainment and not enough in-person connection."

"Social media is an illusion of connection. The youngest generation reports people don't care, ghosting them for something better."

"We overextend what we perceive to be our authentic selves into the universe via social media, which creates this illusion to ourselves and others that we are flying high, life is super-duper fantastic. This can lead to a feeling of being lonely because we have nothing to share in real life with others. Our culture seems to believe, by posting our lives online, that we create community and connection. If anything, I think it isolates us even more because we have nothing left to talk about to an actual person who may care."

"Social media is a huge cause . . . people have more 'friends,' but less connection."

"The disintegration of the traditional family structure and traditional Christian values."

"I blame the rise of social media. We are no longer a society that meets face-to-face anymore, but one in which we have 'conversations' that consist of short posts on a social media platform or a few words in a text message. We don't hear people's voices or see their faces when they talk. We don't look people in the eyes and have a conversation; instead, we hide behind a keyboard."

"Connection isn't a shared value."

"People aren't talking about their feelings with others because they are ashamed or are afraid they will be judged."

"We don't know how to talk with each other. We stay in the shallows, or we get angry. We remain unknown and unseen, and we don't see or truly know others."

"Because true human connection takes vulnerability, which is hard for many."

"Over the years, people have been encouraged to become more independent (which is not bad) but also to follow a dogma that 'I can do it alone, and I don't need to depend on others.'"

I was blown away at how similar these answers were: 168 participants across 28 US states and 3 additional countries, and there's a basic agreement that our rise in loneliness is due to social media, a lack of vulnerability, and a genuine lack of relational connection. I guess we have the answer, and I can end the book here, right?

I wish the answer were that simple, but the bigger problem is that we know what the issues are, but we still aren't doing much about it. Why? Is it fear? Apathy? And where does this fear or apathy come from? I believe the lack of response to loneliness is linked to a systematic misunderstanding of the value of human connection, mixed with a fiercely independent streak that directly leads to a selfish, "me-centric" mindset.

The "I Do It!" Independent Spirit

Where does the independent spirit come from? I ask this question of my counseling students during their very first semester. The class is Human Growth and Development, and the pervasive question in this class is the conversation about nurture versus nature: whether we get our attitudes, behaviors, emotional responses, mental acuity, and mental health from genetics (nature) or from the way we were raised, cultural factors, and caregiver responses (nurture). To emphasize just how gray this topic can become, I split my class into two groups and have them prepare a debate. One group focuses on nurture, while the other group focuses on nature. I instruct them to pour themselves into the topic, cite resources, give examples, and share opinions. I give them ninety minutes to plan, research, and discuss and then ninety minutes to debate. I've been teaching this class off and on for the past ten years, and the results are always the same: a stalemate. Why? Because both sides have valid points.

Once the debate is complete, we discuss whether the following scenario is primarily due to nature or nurture:

> You're the parent of a four-year-old girl. It's Sunday morning, and you're getting ready to go to church. In preparation for leaving on time, you laid out your daughter's clothes the night before. This morning, the choice of clothes is not the issue; it's the speed at which she's putting them on. Finally, she's dressed, but she's having a hard time putting on her shoes. Yes, they're Velcro, but that's not the problem. The issue is she can't figure out which shoe goes on which foot. In your haste, you bend down to help, and she reacts by pulling away and saying, "I do it!" As you insist, her reaction gets stronger. She begins to scream, "I DO IT! I DO IT!"

Is the little girl's desire to complete the task a result of nurture or nature? Of course, from our outside perspective, the answer is "yes."

Autonomy (I am able to do this by myself) and interdependence (we do this together) are topics that we don't often consider as the cause of loneliness. These concepts can be illustrated through the example of marriage. Sarah (my wife) and I grew up in what we thought were very similar families. Both of our families were in some form of ministry (e.g., Christian schoolteachers), were actively involved in the church, emphasized hard work and relationship, and the list could go on. Entering the marriage, we thought that our similarities would allow for a smooth transition into married life. We were wrong! Married life was much harder than we initially expected, for a couple of reasons:

1. We brought our independent spirits into the marriage. Instinctively, we thought that the way we were raised was the way it should be, and we didn't have a healthy concept of each other.

2. We didn't understand the importance of the reciprocal relationship between autonomy (self) and interdependence (us), and because of this, significant loneliness crept in.

I'll break down these concepts—and how they contribute to the increase of loneliness—later in this book.

Cultural Norms—the "Shoulds"

Loneliness is not the absence of relationship. That's isolation—the physical separation of both person and relationship. Loneliness can be linked to cultural norms. When I was pursuing my master's degree from Denver Seminary, I worked several jobs to provide for my family. One of those jobs was being an inner-city youth minister at a local community center. There was a diverse population of immigrant families, but the main population this organization served was the Latino/Hispanic population, many of whom immigrated from Central America. Traditionally, this culture, like many others, is very family-centric. Family structures appear to be loving, welcoming, and engaging environments ideal for relationship and community.

My first mistake was assuming that loneliness wasn't a problem in that community. My second mistake was verbalizing that in one of our youth-group meetings. After a night of games and a short Bible study, one of the high school students came up to me to talk. "Mister Mark" (as they called me), "thank you for tonight," Tony stated. "But I'm struggling with something you said."

As he talked, he worked hard to avoid eye contact. "Tony," I said, "help me understand."

"On the outside looking in," Tony told me, "I can see how you'd assume everything is good, but it isn't. I feel very alone." Tony proceeded to tell me how overwhelmed and ignored he felt in his family. As a first-generation American, he was caught between his culture of origin, being loyal to his family, and wanting to be part of the culture he was living in. In Tony's story, multiple factors played a part in compounding his loneliness.

Loneliness knows no cultural bounds. It can and does affect everyone at some point in their journey. Every culture and subculture throughout history has a list of "shoulds" and "should nots"— expectations that you just know without being told—that often overlook the uniqueness and specific needs of individuals. Think about it: What were your shoulds and should nots growing up?

Every household has a culture, and it's made up of many factors, such as race, socioeconomic status, religion, denomination, education, and so on. Your culture directly or indirectly taught you how to view emotions, religion, faith, mental health, and relationships, and that plays a direct role in your present struggle with loneliness.

The question becomes: How do we respect culture while eradicating loneliness? This will take intentionality, vulnerability, and reflection.

Conclusion

I'm sure many of us can relate to Tre and Tony. We've all experienced loneliness to some degree and have a basic framework for what it feels like. Our personal experiences and perceptions might vary, but there's commonality in the fact that most, if not all, of us have experienced some form of "being alone."

For this book, I believe it's important to have a baseline definition of loneliness. You may have your own definition, but I want to give you mine so that we can be on the same page moving forward into the following chapters. I define *loneliness* as:

> The state of being unseen or unnoticed relationally,
> mentally, emotionally, physically, or spiritually. It can
> be driven by lack of purpose or meaning, relationship,
> and/or identity and is marked by a deep sense of
> hopelessness.

You picked up this book for a reason, and I'm grateful you're joining me in this exploratory conversation. Something systematically must change; we must confront the mental, emotional, physical, and spiritual roots of loneliness. If we don't—or if we choose to ignore the warning signs within us and within our communities—this crisis will continue to worsen, and precious lives will be lost.

Let's explore answers together. I'm passionate about this conversation, and I'm willing to take the risk of starting it. Thank you for joining me! What I will ask as you read this book is that you stay humble, teachable, and vulnerable. Take time to ask questions and reflect, wrestle with this conversation, and allow it to change you where necessary.

Questions for Reflection

1. What's your experience with loneliness been?

2. How would you answer the questions from my online survey?

    a. On a scale of 1 (not lonely) to 5 (very lonely), how lonely do you feel on a daily basis?

    b. In your own words, how would you define *loneliness*?

    c. When you feel lonely, what do you typically do to feel better?

    d. Why do you think loneliness is on the rise in our culture?

    e. If you had a magic wand and could fix the loneliness around you, what would you do?

3. Who else in your life should be reading this book? Give them a copy, and read it with them.

THE PERSONAL COST
OF LONELINESS

Mental, Emotional, Physical, and Spiritual Health

*Depression on my left, Loneliness on my right. They don't need
to show me their badges. I know these guys very well.*

ELIZABETH GILBERT

Over time, loneliness gets inside you and doesn't go away.

CARLOS RUIZ ZAFÓN

WE ALL HAVE A MOMENT that changes our life forever. Mine
happened February 17, 2020. That morning started out like any
other. I got up early, grabbed a cup of coffee, and sat down in
my office to begin working on my day's to-do list. I was in the
midst of organizing my desk when my phone rang. I looked down
and noticed it was my mom calling. *Why would she be calling at
6:00 a.m.?* I wondered.

Then I remembered, and my heart sank. Four days earlier, my
dad had had "routine" prostate cancer surgery. The surgery went
well, and the doctor said he had to take a little more margin (the
area around the tumor to ensure that all the cancer is cleared) than
originally thought but was convinced that everything would be

fine. "I've done hundreds of these surgeries without any mistakes," he quipped with a smile. The next day, my dad was released from the hospital and on his way to recovery.

Panicked, I picked up the phone. "Mom? What's going on?"

"Your dad isn't doing well," my mom said. "He isn't feeling any better, his abdomen hurts, and he can't stand up straight." Her voice quivered a little as she said, "He's in a lot of pain." They were going to wait until the doctor's office opened to get a checkup.

Normally, I would have agreed with her, but he'd already been to the ER forty-eight hours earlier with high pain levels in his abdomen. "Mom, I don't think you should wait." I said, "Go to the ER, and I'll meet you there."

I jumped in the car to make the thirty-minute drive north. When I arrived at the hospital, I immediately knew something was wrong with my dad. He was usually a very active and healthy individual who worked out on a regular basis, but the man in front of me could hardly stand up. He was in excruciating pain and was a slight shade of yellow. The ER nurses and doctors began their standardized procedures to figure out what was causing the pain. After hours of tests, the results were still inconclusive, and they decided to keep him overnight for observation.

Once in his hospital room, he was able to meet with a surgeon who specialized in internal medicine. "We can do one more test," he said. "A CT scan with contrast might show us what we need to see." (A CT scan with contrast is where they inject a dye into the body to see if anything is out of place or leaking.) Twenty minutes after the CT scan, the doctor came back and told us that my dad's bowel had been nicked in the prostate-cancer surgery, and he was going septic. This meant he was slowly dying from the inside out.

As they were rushing him into surgery, I felt a wave of panic come over me. *Will this be the last time I see him? What do I say to him?* As he was being wheeled off, all I could say was "I love you, Dad! See you when you're done." I quickly told myself that everything was going to be okay. Knowing the surgery would take some time, I left the hospital to get dinner with a close friend.

Around 9:00 p.m., my friend dropped me back off at the hospital. As I was walking into the surgery waiting room, my sister called and told me to hurry back. "Dad aspirated on the table, and they're trying to stabilize his vitals. It doesn't look good." I rushed back into the waiting room and sat with my mom, uncle, and sister for what seemed like an eternity.

Finally, just after midnight, the doctor came out. "Your dad is very sick," he said. "He has a serious infection and is in critical condition. We're moving him to the ICU."

"When can we see him?" I asked.

"I can take you there now," the doctor said, "but you need to be prepared. He's on a ventilator because he can't breathe on his own right now, and he's hooked up to a lot of machines, all with the purpose of keeping him alive."

Though I had the warning, I was not prepared to see my dad in that helpless state. Little did we know how long his journey to healing would be. What was meant to be one simple surgery turned into five surgeries to correct the effects of the first. One weekend in the hospital turned into over a month.

My dad spent eight days in the ICU, where we prayed and hoped God would let us keep him. With each long day, the prayers of his family and friends were felt, and Dad started to slowly make steps toward recovery. After thirty days or so in the hospital, he was moved to a rehab center. And after fifteen days in rehab, Dad was released to come home.

It's June 2020 as I write this, and we were finally able to have my parents over for dinner. Dad is still weak and has a big uphill battle, but he's alive, and for that, I'm grateful. I share this story for a couple of reasons. First, I know what it feels like to be in the depths of loneliness. Spending the night with my dad in the ICU, I faced fear, anxiety, depression, anger, and confusion. I felt helpless, hopeless, and alone. Second, I did a lot of observing while I was in the hospital. I realized I was surrounded by loneliness, and it got me thinking, *What are the effects of loneliness? Is mental, emotional, physical, and spiritual distress the cause of loneliness? Or is loneliness the cause of mental, emotional, physical, and spiritual distress?*

Mental Health

It was the fall of 2014, and I was working in a community mental health facility. I was required to have a caseload of eighty to one hundred clients and see them as often as possible, but I was only allowed to work forty hours a week. Overtime wasn't allowed. You're probably doing the math in your head: I could only see my clients once every two to two-and-a-half weeks. Therapeutic care wasn't excellent. What could I do to make a difference with that kind of limited time?

During that time, my wife started looking for a counselor to help her work through some residual trauma from her fight with childhood leukemia. She called seven counselors and never received a call back. These experiences got me thinking, *There has to be a better way. There has to be a way to call people back, to schedule appointments quickly, and to treat people with respect and dignity, not as a number.* We started dreaming and planning.

July 15, 2015, Mayfield Counseling opened its doors for our

community. In five years, we've grown to one of the largest counseling centers in Colorado Springs, with twenty-five counselors, six to eight interns, and two to three support staff. When people call, we pick up the phone, we listen, and we do our best to provide tailored care. In 2019, we did nearly twenty thousand appointments, and in 2020, we were able to top that by about 10 percent. Our eyes were opened to the needs around us, and we're doing what we can to walk with our community.

One thing I've noticed since 2015 is that mental health struggles are significantly rising. Jean Twenge, in her book *iGen: Why Today's Super-Connected Kids Are Growing Up Less Rebellious, More Tolerant, Less Happy—and Completely Unprepared for Adulthood—and What That Means for the Rest of Us*, stated that there was a significant increase in depressive symptoms among high school boys and girls between 2012 and 2015. Boys' depressive symptoms increased by 21 percent, girls' increased by 50 percent, and depression and anxiety are still rising.[1] Furthermore, a survey of new college freshmen indicated that between 2009 and 2016, the severity of student mental health concerns increased significantly. There was an 18 percent increase in rating emotional health below average, a 51 percent increase in feeling overwhelmed, a 64 percent increase in anticipating a need for counseling, and a 95 percent increase in experiencing depressive symptoms.[2]

The *Anxiety and Depression Association of America* indicate that

- 40 million adults struggle with anxiety[3];
- 17.3 million of those eighteen and older have had a major depressive episode in the last year[4]; and
- 2.8 million 12- to 17-year-olds will have a major depressive episode in the next year.[5]

If you do the math, you'll know that is 60.1 million individuals—36.8 percent of the population—who admit to struggling with anxiety and/or depression. That equals approximately one in five in the United States.

These statistics don't take into consideration the other mental illnesses that people may wrestle with daily, such as panic disorders, OCD, PTSD, bipolar disorder, schizophrenia, and many more. Bottom line: More and more people are struggling with mental health, and year after year, mental health struggles are continuing to rise.

A critical theme permeating our mental health culture is the fight against suicide. Suicide is the tenth leading cause of death in the United States. In 2018, approximately 48,000 individuals died by suicide, and in 2019, 1.4 million adults attempted suicide. The age-adjusted suicide rate is 14.2 per one hundred thousand,[6] and on average, 132 individuals die by suicide every day.[7]

Mental illness is hard enough without the backdrop of a culture bent toward superficial connection but practical isolation. Experiencing mental illness causes us to withdraw from one another, and the loneliness that ensues takes a toll on our mental health. No wonder the rates of depression and anxiety are increasing—they subject us to a vicious cycle with no easy off-ramp.

For me, it was the second semester of my sixth-grade year. I was twelve years old. I should've been looking forward to middle school, but instead, I was preoccupied with the severity of my migraine headaches. They'd come out of nowhere two weeks after Christmas break and landed like a ton of bricks. At first, my parents made me go to school, but after a while, the pain became so bad I couldn't concentrate, let alone keep my eyes open in a lit room. My parents pulled me out of school and began setting up appointments with doctors to determine the cause of my pain.

Little did we know my pain wasn't medical but, rather, the effects of internalizing my mental and emotional pain from being bullied at school.

Somewhere between March and April of that year, I broke. I was tired of the physical pain. I was tired of the constant poking and prodding from the doctors. I was tired of the continued bullying and abuse from my peers at school. So one night, after I tried to cry myself to sleep, I went downstairs and ingested a bottle of acetaminophen pills. I walked back upstairs and lay in bed, hoping I wouldn't wake up in the morning.

Not fifteen minutes later, I woke up with a stabbing pain in my stomach. I screamed in agony, and my parents came running. They rushed me to the hospital, where my stomach was pumped. I'm sure the hospital had protocol for my situation because my parents took me to see a psychologist a few days later. That was the moment my journey to healing began. My counselor realized quickly that my physical pain was a manifested symptom of my mental and emotional pain. When the source was properly treated, the physical symptoms started to go away.

Sadly, my story isn't unique. Hundreds of thousands—if not millions—of people walk around with a "physical ailment" that isn't really a physical ailment. I've found, over the years, that everything is connected: There's a direct link between mental, emotional, and physical health. Everything that is psychological is physiological. Depression, anxiety, and suicide are rising rapidly, and in most cases, these struggles can be traced back to loneliness and lack of connection and relationship.

Emotional Health

How do you take someone's emotional pulse? Emotional intelligence or "EQ" has been a hot topic for over a decade, but what is it, and what does it have to do with loneliness?

Basically, EQ is being aware of one's own emotions, being able to pick up on someone else's emotions, and having skills to engage in interpersonal relationships. It is defined as "the capacity to be aware of, control, and express one's emotions, and to handle interpersonal relationships judiciously and empathically."[8] Seems simple enough, right? Then why, as a society, are we failing miserably at it?

Babies are born with the capacity for emotions such as joy, happiness, fear, and shyness. Emotional intelligence, however, develops from the type of nurturing a child is given. A nurturing environment gives a child a 25-percent-greater chance of success in life; a child in a neglectful environment has a 25-percent-lower chance of success.[9]

If you absorb this statistic, it should move you to tears. Early on in my job at the community mental health center, I received a ten-year-old client. This young boy had just been removed from his mom's home due to neglect and abuse. Thankfully, he was placed in the care of his aunt and uncle. During our first couple of sessions, I observed his posture: He was hunched over, with his shoulders rounded and his head facing down. His aunt confirmed that his only possession was an old handheld video-game console. He used video games to pass the time when he was left home alone to fend for himself. His aunt also mentioned that he was struggling to focus on simple tasks and was failing at school.

Over the course of several months, I was privileged to work with the family and establish routines and patterns to support growth. With patience and persistence, we began to see significant changes.

His physical posture straightened, he was able to hold conversations while looking others in the eyes, he was starting to improve in school, and he began to develop friends. The nurturing by his aunt and uncle was starting to reverse years of neglect and abuse.

Our presence and our actions have so much power over our children and their future emotional health. Your socioeconomic status, whether you live in an apartment or a mansion, whether you live in the northern hemisphere or the southern hemisphere, or whether you are a Broncos fan or a Raiders fan really doesn't matter (although I might question your choices if you root for a team other than the one I support). What matters is your presence.

Presence has power—more power than many of us realize. A memory comes to mind from my early years as a dad. I lost my cool with my oldest daughter, who was about three or four at the time. She did something that didn't fit my paradigm of how a three- or four-year-old should act, and I reacted poorly. I remember watching her eyes change and lose their sparkle. Her physical demeanor altered as her shoulders slumped and her head bowed in defeat. It stopped me cold in my tracks. I was a counselor; I should know better! I immediately got down on my knees in front of her and, with tears in my eyes, told her I'd messed up and asked for her forgiveness.

What if I hadn't done this? What if my pride had kept me from modeling emotional intelligence? Could I have contributed to her future loneliness? Sadly, this is the case for many individuals, and the cycle becomes perpetuated from generation to generation. We were created as relational beings. If we miss the vital nurturing needed to grow into emotional intelligence, the intelligence that is reflective of our Creator, we suffer. (In chapter 5, we'll talk about how we're hardwired for connection.)

Mental and emotional health are like conjoined twins. You can't separate them, as they're symbiotically reliant on each other. Yes, they have unique attributes and distinct personalities, but they rely on each other for strength. When one falters, the other suffers too. Our culture doesn't seem to understand this necessary relationship. We can blame media, politicians, food, or screens. Yes, these things can be a contributing factor to the bigger picture, but emotional intelligence and health must be taught in the home.

If we're going to change culture, we must take a hard look at ourselves, our families, and our homes. We must ask ourselves, *What is the mental and emotional state of my home? What are the mental and emotional awareness and intelligence of my home? Am I contributing to or detracting from the overall health of my home?* These are difficult questions that require a measure of vulnerability and self-awareness to accurately assess. I'll talk in Part III about how to create an emotionally and mentally intelligent home. It takes work, but it's worth the effort: I believe that where an individual and a family have mental and emotional health and intelligence, loneliness is hard to find.

Physical Health

Sitting in the ICU with my father, I was astonished at just how sterile the environment was. I guess I shouldn't have been surprised—I was in a hospital, after all. A place where health and healing are fought for and promoted, right? During my many days there, I had ample time to observe. I started to realize that modern medicine works at "scientifically" keeping people alive, but the quality of that life is questionable.

Walking into the ICU, I noticed that many of the patients on life support had no one in the room with them. The individuals with family or friends present had someone by their side twenty-four seven, and they seemed to get better faster and leave the ICU sooner than the others. More questions started to form. Does loneliness affect how we heal, and does it affect our immune systems as well as our mental health? I did some research. This year, approximately 647,000 people will die from heart disease[10] and 606,520 people will die from cancer.[11] The potential connections between loneliness and health should not be ignored.

Stress

Stress is an all-too-familiar feeling and a word that is thrown around in a variety of scenarios. What is stress, and how is it linked to loneliness? Stress is the body's natural response to external stimuli or pressure. When we are affected by an outside stimulus, our body releases a steroid hormone called cortisol. Cortisol, which is produced in the cortex of the adrenal gland, keeps us aroused and alert in times of stress. When cortisol is released, it activates the sympathetic nervous system, which increases heart rate, which increases blood flow to major muscle groups. It dilates our pupils, which allows us to take in more light and see better, slows or stops digestion, stimulates adrenal glands for sudden bursts of energy and mental clarity, and constricts blood vessels to minimize blood loss in case of injury. Once the sympathetic nervous system does its job and we've addressed the stress-inducing situation, the parasympathetic nervous system kicks in and brings everything back to equilibrium. Effectually, our bodies were kicked into fight-or-flight mode (stress mode) and then brought back into homeostasis.

There's "good stress" and "bad stress." Cortisol can be a good automatic response when we're challenged with studying for a test, preparing for the big game, training for a marathon, or getting out of a sticky situation. "Bad stress" is the same process as "good stress" without the parasympathetic nervous system being activated to calm things down. The individual becomes stuck in fight-or-flight mode, which has deleterious effects on their brain and body. The cortisol spigot is left on and begins to eat away at their body's integrity. Adrenal fatigue, inflammation, and a weakened immune system are a few of the complications that can arise. Prolonged stress can even shrink the brain.

These effects can be passed down from generation to generation as the way a person under stress nurtures and affects the attachment bonds—the initial and ongoing connection between child and caregiver—between the child and parent. If there's a weakened attachment bond, the child does not learn proper coping skills for stress and, as a result, develops fewer cortisol receptors in the brain, which hinders the child from properly dealing with stress-producing situations.

Sleep

Sleep is meant to be regenerative. When we sleep, our bodies rest and our cells literally repair themselves. When we're asleep, our bodies are very much awake.

As I write this, my imagination is running wild, and I'm recalling a scene from the Disney/Pixar film *Inside Out*. The characters Joy and Sadness are stranded, trying to find their way back to headquarters. As they walk through long-term memory, workers are cleaning up old or discarded memories. This is what "should" happen to us when we're asleep. Recent research shows that there is a direct correlation between quality of social relationships and the psychological and physiological repair process in sleep.[12]

Simply put, the lonelier someone is, the weaker their sleep patterns are. The weaker the sleep patterns, the weaker the psychological and physiological repair processes—and, subsequently, the immune system.

Circulatory System and the Heart

Don't tune out. I know, the title of this section seems a bit strange and "scientific," but hang in there with me. A dear friend of mine recently introduced me to Dr. Thomas Cowan, whose book *Human Heart, Cosmic Heart: A Doctor's Quest to Understand, Treat, and Prevent Cardiovascular Disease* challenges the notion that the heart is only a pump. It has a deeper, holistic, and more complex purpose than previously thought:

> When blood exits the heart, it travels through the large aortic arch into the major arteries and then into the small arterioles until it meets the "midpoint," that is, the capillaries.
>
> Capillaries are the one-layer thick transition vessels where nutrients and gases are exchanged between the blood and the cells. The capillary system is massive; if it were spread out, it would cover at least one entire football field. After the blood exits the capillaries, it enters the smallest venules in its trip back to the heart. From the small venules, it goes to the progressively larger veins and then finally into the largest veins like the inferior and superior vena cava that bring all of the blood back from the body to the heart and lungs. The purpose of this circulation is to bring oxygenated, nutrient-rich blood to the cells where it is needed and then bring the

oxygen-poor, nutrient-poor blood back to the heart and lungs so that it can be replenished.[13]

Are you still with me? The circulatory system cycles "good" or "healthy" oxygen-rich blood filled with nutrients to cells in the body and then takes depleted blood cells back to the heart and lungs to be replenished. This all makes sense, right? Cowan takes it a step further:

> Blood actually stops moving in the capillaries, which is necessary for the efficient exchange of gases, nutrients, and waste products. After the blood stops moving, it oscillates slightly, and then begins to flow again as it enters the veins. But if the blood stops moving at the midpoint of its circular flow through the blood vessels, only then to start moving again, what is the force that drives this movement of the blood from its motionless state before it leaves the capillaries and begins its journey back to the heart? Is it possible that this force is the "pumping" of the heart? Wouldn't there have to be some pump located in the capillaries propelling the blood forward and upward? Is there some "vital" force located in the capillaries that does this pumping? . . . The force cannot come from the heart. It must arise in the capillaries.[14]

Cowan goes on to describe how the principles of structured water—a form of water that sits on the surface of "bulk" (or normal) water—apply to the functions of the capillaries. Structured water is also referred to as EZ water or exclusion zone water; it has negatively charged ions and sits above bulk water, which has positively charged ions. Capillaries are essentially a hydrophilic, or water-loving, tube, with structured water close to the tube lining and bulk water in the middle (see Figure 2).

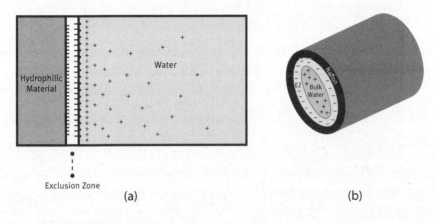

Cowan states:

> Within this tube, something astounding happens. As a result of the separation of electrical charges—again, the natural and inevitable consequence of the interaction of a hydrophilic tube and water—the bulk water will begin to flow from one end of the tube to the other and then out. Furthermore, this flow will be indefinite, unless acted upon by a force that stops it.[16]

Essentially, due to the relative position of positively and negatively charged ions, the blood in capillaries can stop, oscillate, release nutrients and oxygen, then start again on its own. How creative is our God!

But what does this have to do with loneliness? Loneliness

and lack of secure relationships have been shown to significantly increase the risk of cardiovascular disease, including high blood pressure and coronary heart disease.[17] What if the force that Cowan discussed is actually the essential need for connection? And what if the health of our circulator system is linked to the depth and quality of our relationships?

Various research correlates with this "what if" by indicating that hopelessness, a component of loneliness, predicts mortality rates in older adults and hospital patients with cardiovascular distress. Furthermore, there is a higher rate of cardiac arrest in those in the general population with coronary artery disease.[18] The health of our connectedness directly affects the health of our circulatory system. A "lack of secure relationships and loneliness are associated with greater risk of developing cardiovascular disease."[19]

We are uniquely designed and created to be in a healthy symbiotic relationship with Someone Else, and it directly affects our physiology. If that doesn't blow your mind, I'm not sure what will. (This is also linked to quantum energy, which we'll discuss further in a later chapter.)

The Road Heavily Traveled: Predisease Pathways

Many years ago, Fran sought me out to work on her anxiety and depression. It'd become so bad that she didn't know where else to turn. After several sessions, Fran revealed that she'd been struggling with neuropathy from the knees down. (Neuropathy is where you slowly lose feeling in your extremities due to deteriorating nerves. It can be very painful.) She'd been going to doctors and specialists to find a cure, or at least some relief, but hadn't had any luck. We figured out that this was a contributing factor to her anxiety and depression, but I was uncertain this was the core issue.

Several sessions later, we discovered the core. Fran disclosed she was in an abusive work relationship with her boss. This relationship created an insurmountable amount of stress, which was directly linked to her anxiety and depression.

Through several sessions of counseling, Fran decided to quit her job. I'll never forget the phone call I received several days later. "Mark!" a voice quivering exclaimed. "This is Fran."

"Hi! How are you?" I asked.

"Good. I mean, really good! I quit my job today!"

"Wonderful!" I exclaimed. "How are you feeling?"

"Well, that's the funny thing. I hung up the phone with my boss, and the feeling in my legs came back!"

We both sat there in silence for a moment, then Fran started to laugh, and we celebrated over the phone what had just happened. I'm not a medical doctor, but that was an amazing experience—a miracle, even. I was intrigued by this and wondered if other ailments could be healed in similar ways. In fact, this story sparked my curiosity and later led me to begin writing this book.

During my research, I stumbled on a concept called *predisease pathways*, or the biological influences and related links to behavioral, psychological, and social influences that precede sickness and death. What I found fascinating was how predisease pathways pertain to loneliness and relationships. Loneliness and social isolation can be predictive of sickness and life expectancy, even after controlling for health factors such as exercise and nutrition.[20] Loneliness directly contributes to the inflammation or excitation of chronic diseases such as cancer, cardiovascular disease, affective disorders, drug or alcohol abuse, chronic obstructive pulmonary disease, sleep disorders, diabetes, and dementia. This means loneliness is a major predisease pathway, an interstate thoroughfare to sickness. Fran could attest that her interpersonal struggles were directly linked to both psychological and physical ailments.

Spiritual Health

Loneliness doesn't just affect our physical health; it also has an impact on spiritual health, as we see from The Genesis account of the Fall. I'm fascinated by the lack of creativity of the serpent and the obliviousness of many of us in the church. Reflect on Genesis 3. Was the serpent's lie about the fruit, or was it about questioning Adam and Eve's relationship with God? In Genesis 3:4-5, the serpent challenges God's relational intent, attempting to triangulate the relationship between Adam, Eve, and God through miscommunication:

> You won't die. God knows that the moment you eat from
> that tree, you'll see what's really going on. You'll be just
> like God, knowing everything, ranging all the way from
> good to evil.

Think about the subtleties of this lie. Eve had assumed eating from that tree would result in physical death; the serpent knowingly used the word for spiritual and relational death (loneliness and separation). Eve repeated what God had asked of them; the serpent insinuated God was keeping something of value from them. Obviously, physical death didn't happen immediately or in the way Eve had originally thought; rather, spiritual and relational death and separation ensued from eating of the forbidden tree. I see threads of this lie throughout our modern church as minor differences or disagreements deepen the divide—and increase the separation, isolation, and loneliness that entered the world with the Fall.

If loneliness and isolation are rising, then the importance of collaborative community within the church must be declining. Why? Because if one of the original intents of the church was to develop authentic community whereby individuals would engage in the mutual redemptive work of the gospel, wouldn't the lie of loneliness significantly affect and hinder this work? The lonelier we are (or perceive we are), the less likely we are to engage in community. The less likely we are to engage in community, the less likely we are to commit to a church, a prayer life, or a life engaged in Scripture—each of which forces a lonely individual to confront difficult life areas and make changes, which in turn requires relationship and community. Loneliness directly decreases spiritual health and relational community because it's a blatant repurposing of the original lie. Without community rooted in the gospel, we lose all ability to recognize truth.

Wrapping It Up

It can be overwhelming to consider the many effects of loneliness and the specific complications therein. Take some time to reflect. Maybe this chapter has confirmed what you already know or have suspected all along. Or maybe this chapter has completely blown your mind and has started you down the path of reevaluating your mental, emotional, physical, and spiritual health.

Wherever you are in this journey of revelation, that's okay. I encourage you not to brush off or gloss over this content. Instead, sit with it, explore the emotions that arise, and write down what you are thinking and feeling. Use the reflection questions below as a guide.

Questions for Reflection

1. What are your initial "gut" reactions to this chapter? What surprised you?

2. On a scale of 1 to 10, where 1 means unhealthy and 10 means thriving, how would you rate and describe your mental, emotional, physical, and spiritual health?

3. In what ways can you begin to change some of these areas?

THE CULTURAL CONUNDRUM
Success, Technology, and Tribalism

A fixation with connecting with "friends" online comes with the risk of disconnection with friends waiting for you to be present in the offline world.

CRAIG HODGES

Being connected to everything has disconnected us from ourselves and the preciousness of this present moment.

L. M. BROWNING

THERE'S NO DOUBT that loneliness has destructive effects on our mental, emotional, physical, and spiritual health, but do we ever pay attention to the contributing factors of loneliness? What I mean is: Are we giving credence to the things that are deepening this loneliness epidemic? Three key contributing problems make this loneliness epidemic worse: (1) our definition of success, (2) our reliance on screens, and (3) our yearning to belong to something bigger than ourselves. These three things complicate the insidious nature of loneliness.

The Lie of Success

How would you define success? Many of us have never thought about it, yet success has a way of directing, if not ruling, every aspect of our lives.

This mindset is something I fell into early on in my career. Upon graduating from Colorado Christian University with a BA in youth ministry, I embarked on my journey to become a youth pastor. Eight months after graduation, I was hired to be the youth and family pastor of a small church in a bustling Colorado mountain town. Several months into starting the job, I became intimately aware of several ministries doing similar work there. A wiser or more mature person probably would have looked for ways to collaborate with these organizations. I, on the other hand, looked for ways to compete.

I became obsessed with performance, and I compared our numbers at weekly gatherings and monthly events to the other organizations' numbers. If I had more kids attending than the place down the street did, I was a success; if I didn't, I was a failure. I became consumed with making the biggest and the best impact, and I lost sight of the real importance of ministry. My definition of success infiltrated every aspect of me and my work, and I jumped on the roller coaster of emotions that eventually led to bitterness, isolation, comparison, and loneliness.

Looking back on my time at that ministry, I realize just how miserable I was. The more I leaned into my definition of success, the more isolated I became. I missed out on amazing relationships and ignored collaboration that could've had a deeper, more lasting impact on the community.

I wonder how many of you can relate. If we don't explore our own paradigms of success, they'll infiltrate our daily lives and ruin how we operate.

What is the world's current definition of success? What messages are being communicated to you and your family? Far too often, I hear that success is a specific formula, such as

Good Grades + Talent + Popularity = Success
or
Good Job + Money + Things = Success

Maybe these definitions will suffice for the time being, but when does "more" or "better" take precedent over "enough"?

Keeping Up with the Joneses

"Keeping up with the Joneses." We've all heard it; my wife hates it. Her maiden name is Jones, and she's frustrated and somewhat embarrassed when people use the phrase to compare statuses. Truth is we live in a world where comparison is everything. How do I measure up to my neighbor, my friends, my _____? Am I wearing the most up-to-date fashion? Is my car newer than _____'s car? Am I driving the right model? The right brand? Is my house in the right neighborhood? The list could go on and on.

Consistent, continual comparison to others can plant a seed of jealousy which, if left unattended, can lead to a root of bitterness toward others and create discontent within ourselves. These two things combined create a relational rift internally and between us and others. If this isn't confronted and dealt with, it'll directly contribute to us becoming disconnected and lonely. In fact, the loneliness we feel will only worsen.

Several years ago, I did an intake session with parents who were concerned about their son's success in school. Sitting down with both the mom and dad, I could sense their worry. I typically meet with parents prior to meeting with the child. This allows me to assess the bigger picture and develop a preliminary treatment plan. In this case, the parents indicated that their son's grades had been slipping and that his social acting-out behaviors might hinder him from entering an Ivy League school.

Throughout the intake session, I had assumed several things:

1. that the parents had communicated their expectations to their child;
2. that their child aspired to attend an Ivy League school; and
3. that their child was in high school.

I was wrong on all three. As we were wrapping up the session, I asked whether their child would be driving himself to the next session to meet with me one-on-one. Both parents looked at me with confusion and chuckled. "Our child is in kindergarten." I pride myself on having a pretty good poker face, but I couldn't hide my disbelief in that moment.

Sadly, this story is far too common. Maybe you felt this way growing up. Maybe as you read this, you're realizing you've done something similar with your children. Whatever the realization, we must honestly reflect on how success is viewed, defined, and communicated in our families and within ourselves. If not, these unspoken expectations and definitions of success will begin to eat away at our family members' confidence and identity, thus deepening and exacerbating the innate struggle with loneliness.

Social Media, Screens, and the Overindulgence of Information

Another important contributing factor to the epidemic of loneliness is our dependence on social media and screens. Before you dismiss this as only a problem for young people, ask yourself, *When was the last time I looked at my phone, checked my social media accounts, read the news, checked recipes, and the like online?* Whether it's Facebook, Instagram, Snapchat, Twitter, WhatsApp, or other social media platforms, screens and social media can be all-consuming. Those of you with an Apple device receive weekly reports on your screen time. Admittedly, I spend too much time on my device (especially during this pandemic), and I'm convicted as I write this!

When I was a kid in the 1980s and 1990s, the parenting craze was to not let your kid watch too much television. But that was it! We didn't have personal computers or laptops, and mobile phones weren't really a thing. Not to mention you had to get off the couch and walk across the living room to change the channel or adjust the volume. I can't tell you how excited I was as a kid when we got a television with a remote.

Now, everything is at our fingertips. The average American home has 7.3 devices.[1] As I sit here and write this, I count eight digital devices in our home, not including the television. That is a lot of devices! Here are some effects:

1. *Blue-Light Effect:* Light is life. All living things need natural light to survive. Red light (light from the sun) is made up of many color wavelengths, and it controls our sleep-wake cycle, known as our circadian rhythm, through the distribution of a hormone called melatonin. Its production peaks at nighttime, when it's circulated throughout our body, signaling that it's time to sleep.[2] Blue light (artificial light emitted from the devices we use) negatively affects melatonin production. The more time we spend on our devices, the less melatonin production and the less likely we are to have regenerative sleep. Without regenerative sleep, our immune system is weaker.

2. *Brain Development:* The brain is a complex organ that's always adapting and changing (in Part II, we'll talk about how God designed our brains for connection). Too much screen time can adversely affect the brain's ability to grow. NewYork-Presbyterian medical center reports on some ongoing research: "Early data from a landmark National Institute for Health study that began in 2018 indicates that children who spent more than two hours a day on screen-time activities scored lower on language and think-ing tests, and some children with more than seven hours a day of screen time experienced thinning of the brain's cortex, the area of the brain related to critical thinking and reasoning."[3] Overuse of screens can also stunt social and relational maturity as well as emotional development.

3. *Mental Health:* As we discussed in the previous chapter, anxiety and depression have been significantly increasing since 2007 and the advent of the smartphone.

4. *Social and Relational Arrested Development:* Arrested development is the phenomenon whereby an individual stops developing or regresses in development. This topic has been the plotline of a popular cable TV show and the punch line of many jokes, yet it's a real problem when it comes to overuse of screens. It's as if we've forgotten how to have a conversation or we just don't remember how to regulate ourselves when we're in a one-on-one exchange. Overuse of screens results in underuse of social, emo-tional, and relational skills. As with brain development, if we don't use it, we lose it. When we don't engage in face-to-face interactions on a regular basis, we lose the ability

to recognize and respond to facial cues, voice tone and inflection, body language, and the energy of emotions in the room. When we lose these relational skills, we become lonelier.

5. *Lack of Inhibition:* Have you ever said something you regretted? What happened? What was the other person's reaction? How did you feel as you said it? For those of us who grew up prior to the 2000s, these types of conversations and conflicts happened in person. We had to look the person in the eyes and work through the struggle, deal with the uncomfortable feelings, wrestle with the emotions, and figure out a resolution. Behind a screen, we seemingly can do or say anything we want because we don't have that immediate relational feedback that occurs when we are face-to-face. In 2015, psychologist Marion Underwood and sociologist Robert Faris tracked and analyzed approximately 150,000 social media posts from more than 200 eighth graders.[4] What they found turned into the CNN documentary *#Being 13*, and the results were astounding.[5] This group of thirteen-year-olds effectually created drastically different online personas for themselves. Media theorist Douglass Ruskoff calls this *digiphrenia*, which is "the experience of trying to exist in more than one incarnation of yourself at the same time."[6] The studied thirteen-year-olds felt the freedom to do or say whatever they wanted online, without fear of consequence or repercussion. This phenomenon affects adults as well. If you don't believe me, just scroll on social media and look at some of the comments people leave.

Tribalism

Have you ever had a deep yearning to belong? So deep you would do or say *anything* to be part of something? As I ask these questions, I feel this yearning in the pit of my stomach. It feels like butterflies fluttering around. It's a mixture of fear and excitement, an unknown up ahead, and a deep longing. I'm also holding my breath, waiting for something, something big to happen, something of importance. I've felt this my whole life. Maybe you have, too, but you haven't been able to put your finger on it. We aren't taught to recognize or even talk about it. So it sits inside us, ruminating, growing in passion and strength, until it bursts out of us.

Most often, it does so in unhealthy ways. As I reflect on my middle school years, I realize that this happened to me. As I previously mentioned, I struggled deeply with loneliness, to the point that I didn't see the purpose of living. I was able to rise out of that deep pit of darkness and despair, yet my mindset didn't fully change. My intense loneliness had dissipated some, but my desire to belong, to fit in, to be part of the club, and to be valued didn't change. In fact, it grew bigger, and I became more desperate to achieve it.

In ninth grade, I finally fit in, but in order to do so, I became something I thought I would never become: a bully. I knew what it felt like to be bullied, but my desire to fit in was stronger than my dislike of bullying. I went to a small Christian school in northern Colorado. I was one of fifteen students, so the dynamics were a bit interesting. A class that size would make for a good social experiment. I'm sure the experiment would find that the majority opinion would win, that coercion, peer pressure, and manipulation would be high, whether intentional or unintentional. I didn't want to be on the receiving end of bullying anymore, so I chose to be on the other end.

I can't remember if I willfully chose to be a bully, but I do remember the moment that it happened. We were in science class, and our teacher was Mrs. Radford. I knew better than to speak out of turn in her class. She was a tough but fair teacher who didn't mess around and kept the class in order. It was when she briefly stepped out to deal with a student that it happened. There was this classmate with a tendency to knock things over, run into things, and make random, sometimes inappropriate, comments. She couldn't help it, but I didn't know that (or, in all honesty, care). When Mrs. Radford was out, this student knocked over a glass beaker full of solvent, and it spilled all over the floor, spreading glass shards everywhere. The entire class stared and laughed. No one moved to help clean up the mess. I seized the opportunity to say, "Good job, klutz. Look at the mess you made." The class—especially the boys I was trying to impress—laughed even harder, and each of them gave me a high five. I was in! But at what cost?

As I reflect on that moment, I can see that girl on the floor, trying to clean up the mess while wiping away tears. No one comforted her or helped her. I feel terrible as I write this, especially knowing it wasn't the last time I did or said something unkind to her. I wish I could go back and apologize, make it right. My desire to belong, to fit in, to be seen outweighed my desire to maintain my morals and my conscience. I can't dismiss my behavior by saying, "It's something kids do," or "My brain wasn't fully developed." It was wrong, and it shouldn't have happened. Unfortunately, it happens all the time.

Tribalism is like a dripping faucet over a rock. Over time, and with consistency, it'll begin to erode a person's sense of true connection and lead to loneliness.

Have you turned on the news lately? It's not good. So much

hate, so much divisiveness. It's become us versus them, you versus me, and it makes sense. Why? Because there's a world of people out there who want to belong, who want to be a part of something bigger than themselves—and who, just like my high school self, are willing to go against their consciences to get there. The desire to fit in outweighs anything else. As this desire grows, emotions increase, and logic goes out the door.

Several things have the potential to happen within us when we go down this path (see Figure 3):

Tribalism Cycle

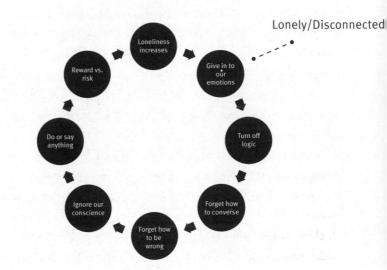

- We give in to our emotions.
- We turn off logic.
- We forget how to have a conversation.
- We forget that it's okay to be wrong.

- We begin to ignore our conscience.
- We do or say anything to fit in or maintain status.
- We see the reward as greater than the risk.
- Loneliness increases significantly.

We Give In to Our Emotions

Emotions are a very powerful force. They can hit us like a tidal wave, knocking us over with their fierceness and velocity. Oftentimes our emotions are not singular but rather multifaceted in nature. They can feel like a ball of tangled Christmas lights, hard to decipher where one strand ends and the other begins. To make matters worse, when you try to untangle them, it can become a frustrating mess that just perpetuates the cycle.

You'll see a perfect visual of this if you watch a three-year-old try to accomplish something new. I can remember when my youngest daughter was three. She went through this growth phase where she wanted to get dressed on her own. One day, she was working on putting on a shirt and was struggling. I knew that trying to step in to help would only make matters worse. So, like any good dad, I stepped back and watched, trying my best not to laugh too hard.

After several calm attempts, she started to get more and more frustrated, then suddenly threw herself on the floor and started kicking and screaming. Her emotions came out of nowhere, like a tidal wave, and took her out. Yes, she was a toddler, and that reaction was very normal and expected. She was in a growth process of development, and it makes complete sense that she would respond that way. Instead of getting frustrated with her, I got down on the floor and said, "It's hard to get dressed by yourself. I'd be mad too." I asked if she needed help and then helped her finish getting dressed. My calm example helped her recognize the importance of emotions, created meaning for her, validated her, and then provided a solution. (Sadly, it remains all too easy to slip into communication with children that can be devastating to them.)

A tribalistic culture feeds on this kind of emotional tidal wave. We stop paying attention to our emotional threshold and willingly cross the line—and we're often celebrated for it. As a result, we regularly see adults throwing tantrums like angry three-year-olds.

I knew I was going to cross a line when I chose to become a bully. I ignored the tidal wave of emotions and willfully crossed that line. The sad thing is those in the "in crowd" didn't care about my emotions or morals. Logic, reasoning, and intellect went out the door, all so I could be part of something and fit in.

We Turn Off Logic

The emotional brain is a reactive brain. When an outside stimulus affects us, our brains and bodies are wired to react. This is how we stay safe and survive. But this process short-circuits the pathway to the prefrontal cortex, the thinking and reasoning part of the brain (we'll talk more about how God designed our brain in Part II). When your emotions take over, logic, intellect, and reasoning turn off.

Have you ever worked with a middle schooler? My dad was a middle school Bible and history teacher for nearly forty years, and he'd joke that middle schoolers feel first and think later. When I talk with parents and youth leaders, I often get asked the question: "How do I help a teen slow down and think through their actions and reactions?" I typically do the counselor thing of answering the question with a question: "What is a teenager's response to the question 'What were you thinking?'" Everyone answers in unison,

"They say, 'I don't know.'" "Right!" I respond. "Because they typically don't know what they're thinking; they're mostly feeling." So I challenge parents and youth leaders to ask their teen what they were feeling so that they can then work backward and help them connect with what they were thinking. We need people in our lives to act as a buffer, to challenge us and our thoughts and feelings, so that we can develop into thoughtful, well-rounded individuals.

When you become part of a tribe, you start to all look, feel, and think the same way, and the "need" for logic goes out the window. Sadly, this applies to adults, as well.

We Forget How to Have a Conversation

I grew up with an Italian extended family. My grandmother on my dad's side was 100 percent Italian, and her parents emigrated from southern Italy to the United States in the early 1900s. As a kid, it was always a treat to travel from northern Colorado to Little Italy on the north side of Denver. When we showed up at my great-aunt's home, there were second cousins, aunts, uncles, food, and a lot of conversation. In fact, there wouldn't just be one conversation but multiple conversations going on at once. If you weren't part of one conversation, you could simply jump in.

It was also chaotic and loud. The more conversations that were happening, the louder it got. There was no waiting your turn to speak; you either interrupted to get your point across or you didn't speak at all. I thought this was the norm for conversations . . . until I got married and quickly realized talking over people wasn't the norm. I must admit that, fourteen years later, I'm still working on this concept: When I get into the heat of a conversation, I can forget to wait my turn.

Reflecting on my experience growing up, I wonder just how

much my family heard. Were we really listening, or were we just trying to get our idea, thought, or opinion out at any cost? This type of "conversation" is more the norm now. When I turn on the news, I scratch my head and wonder if we, as a society, have lost the ability to have a cordial conversation. Everyone wants to be heard, but no one wants to listen. Everyone wants their opinion validated, but no one listens to understand. This is one of the biggest problems with a tribalistic mindset: Every tribe is fighting to have the loudest voice, and no one is willing to listen. Author and journalist George Packer states, "To get along without a tribe makes you a fool. To give an inch to the other tribe makes you a sucker."[7]

We Forget That It's Okay to Be Wrong

Confirmation bias is the phenomenon that people have the conscious or unconscious tendency to seek out information that aligns with their preexisting opinions and ideals. With information at our fingertips, it's much easier to find information that confirms and strengthens our opinion versus information that challenges our opinion.

You might be thinking, *Mark, isn't it a good thing to have access to information?* Yes, it is, but confirmation bias can cause us to forgo logic and, as a result, marginalize truth for the need to be right.

When I was working in the juvenile justice system, a lot of the clients in my group were there for a "minor in possession" charge, MIP for short. Typically, they were charged with possession of a controlled substance, most likely marijuana, and they'd spend much of the first several sessions trying to convince me that marijuana was a healthy choice. Instead of trying to convince them otherwise, I'd challenge them to research the topic and bring some "proof" to our next session.

Inevitably, they'd bring in an article or a social media post. They'd walk in with confidence and drop the article or printed post at my feet and smile, saying, "See, I told you!" Often, these articles or posts were from a marijuana-growers association or another pro-drug source. We would then talk about confirmation bias and how anyone can find anything to make a point. And I'd share medical studies from places like Harvard or Yale and show videos of brains affected by marijuana. I didn't always change their minds, but I did get them thinking.

All of us have aspects of confirmation bias in our lives. It's human nature to seek information that confirms our ideals and beliefs. It's much harder to be vulnerable, aware, and teachable. What is the opposite of being teachable? Pride, or maybe arrogance.

Pride is dangerous because it puffs up our own ideals and mindset, doesn't take into consideration a different point of view, and hardly ever leaves room for being teachable. When we give in to our emotions, forgo logic, and don't know how to have a reciprocal conversation, we allow pride a chance to take root. People who are proud can't admit when they're wrong. Sadly, this mindset is becoming more and more prevalent in our culture.

I recently watched a video of an individual badmouthing a group of people in our culture. The individual stated that if she heard this group say a certain phrase one more time, she was going to cause serious bodily harm and watch them bleed out. Two days later, this individual lost her job due to her intolerant remarks. Instead of owning her mistake, apologizing, and making amends, she blamed the same group of people that she was threatening.

Tribal narratives inflate those in the tribe to a point where their pride in association blinds them to logic and they stay in the swirling mess of their emotions. Being able to admit a wrong-doing and take a humble, teachable stance becomes a foreign concept within the tribe. For example: *If I have to admit that I'm wrong, then I've created a crack in my persona, and my identity is challenged. If my identity is challenged, then I have to confront the question of who I am, and if I can't answer that apart from the tribe, then there's the potential of entering the abyss of loneliness, which can't be an option. So I'll defend my position, even if it's wrong or illogical.*

We Begin to Ignore Our Conscience

If you've been following my train of thought so far, the logical next step is to address turning off our moral compass: our conscience. Early on in my career as a counselor, I worked with youth in the juvenile justice system and gangs from Denver's inner city. Every individual who entered one of my therapy groups was court-ordered to be there, so you can imagine their extreme happiness and desire to participate (insert sarcasm here). I love a challenge, so I'd make it my mission to get them to like therapy. This typically happened week twenty of a twenty-six-week group.

I had this one young man who started out in a gang when he was eight years old. His dad was in jail, and his mom was doing the best she could, considering the circumstances. He told me that the process of becoming a gang member was slow and subtle. "At first, they'd have me run an envelope or a package from one end of the block to the other. They'd reward me with ice cream. The next thing I knew, I was robbing someone at gunpoint." Numbing out our conscience is a similar process. We ignore the small things that cause us to pause; then eventually, we ignore the big things. The innate, ingrained, and created desire to belong will far too often outweigh the desire to be moral and maintain your conscience. At the end of the road, you may have surrounded yourself with "like-minded" people and still feel completely alone. You may ask yourself, *My God, what have I done?*

We Do or Say Anything to Fit In or Maintain Status

If you think about it, the logic behind joining and participating in a tribe is like that of joining and maintaining status in a gang. I became part of a tribe in high school when I chose to cross the line and become a bully. I so desperately wanted to fit in that I was willing to do or say anything to get in, and then I was willing to do or say anything to maintain status. Packer states that "Tribes demand loyalty, and in return they confer the security of belonging."[8] But to what end?

We See the Reward as Greater Than the Risk

Dopamine is a neurotransmitter directly associated with pleasure. It is often known as the "enjoy life" or "natural cocaine" molecule. Practically, when we engage in an activity such as eating, exercising, or being intimate with a spouse, we experience a dopamine release that makes us feel good. Dopamine releases also happen when we get a "like" or a share on social media or try something new outside our comfort zone. The release isn't as great as in other activities, but there's a release nonetheless.

This is one of the reasons why social media and screens can become addicting—and why people stay engaged with a tribe. When you give in to your emotions, forgo logic, ignore your conscience, and become willing to do or say anything, you tend to "up your game" by seeking the next, greater reward. The addictive behavior of seeking reward or pleasure takes over.

This can be exemplified by watching the spring 2020 riots on television in, for example, the "autonomous zone" temporarily established in Seattle to keep police out of a certain neighborhood. Government intervention eventually became necessary due to the violence that ensued. I wonder how many people in this autonomous zone truly believed in the cause—or whether the thrill of a dopamine-and-adrenaline cocktail was what propelled their actions. Human nature, if not confronted, will always search for the next or bigger release. This makes me wonder how much of tribalism is ideologically driven by true passion. Or is it driven solely by the existential desire to be seen, known, valued, and loved?

Loneliness Increases Significantly

When I chose to step into the role of bully in high school, I assumed that those in the "tribe" would become my friends and that I would be seen for the first time and valued for who I was. Sadly, the opposite happened: I went deeper into my loneliness. Tribes become a badge of identity, but they require you to forgo independent reasoning and thought. The group thinks for the individual; independent thinking is actively discouraged, even punished. In a world where connection and relationship are highly coveted, tribe mentality provides a narrative of belonging, however false and flimsy. Whenever we step outside the tribe's boundaries, we're once again confronted with the reality of our loneliness.

Conclusion

It took me a while to realize that I had willfully chosen to participate in the tribe mentality in high school, and I don't fault myself for wanting to fit in. High school can be a difficult time for many working toward identity development.

I finally broke free from the tribe my senior year of high school.

I wish I could give you a three-step process of how to do this, but I can't. What I can say is that I was tired of the drama. I was more confident in who I was becoming, and I chose to place my focus on something else. Breaking free from my own bout with tribalism had more to do with my own mindset than it did with any external circumstances. I had to ask myself, *Am I more concerned with what others think, or am I more concerned with my own integrity and identity?* This was not an easy decision, nor did it provide me with a bunch of friends, but the loneliness shifted. It's hard to explain, but though I was alone after I left the tribe, I was less lonely. The emptiness had lifted. Change takes awareness, and awareness takes vulnerability and honesty. (I'll unpack this idea more in later chapters.)

Loneliness involves many confounding problems. There can be layers on layers of complexity behind feeling alone. In my personal and professional experience, desire for success, emboldened overuse of social media and screens, and participation in a tribe are all distractions from the root cause. They provide a fake sense of purpose and a false narrative that lead many down the path of lies and deceit. Furthermore, the mental, emotional, physical, and spiritual effects of loneliness are undeniably frightening. Yet I take heart in recognizing that this isn't how God intended it to be. John 10:1-18 sheds light on this problem and introduces a different narrative.

> [Jesus said,] "Let me set this before you as plainly as I
> can. If a person climbs over or through the fence of a
> sheep pen instead of going through the gate, you know
> he's up to no good—a sheep rustler! The shepherd walks
> right up to the gate. The gatekeeper opens the gate to him

and the sheep recognize his voice. He calls his own sheep by name and leads them out. When he gets them all out, he leads them and they follow because they are familiar with his voice. They won't follow a stranger's voice but will scatter because they aren't used to the sound of it."

Jesus told this simple story, but they had no idea what he was talking about. So he tried again. "I'll be explicit, then. I am the Gate for the sheep. All those others are up to no good—sheep rustlers, every one of them. But the sheep didn't listen to them. I am the Gate. Anyone who goes through me will be cared for—will freely go in and out, and find pasture. A thief is only there to steal and kill and destroy. I came so they can have real and eternal life, more and better life than they ever dreamed of.

"I am the Good Shepherd. The Good Shepherd puts the sheep before himself, sacrifices himself if necessary. A hired man is not a real shepherd. The sheep mean nothing to him. He sees a wolf come and runs for it, leaving the sheep to be ravaged and scattered by the wolf. He's only in it for the money. The sheep don't matter to him.

"I am the Good Shepherd. I know my own sheep and my own sheep know me. In the same way, the Father knows me and I know the Father. I put the sheep before myself, sacrificing myself if necessary. You need to know that I have other sheep in addition to those in this pen. I need to gather and bring them, too. They'll also recognize my voice. Then it will be one flock, one Shepherd. This is why the Father loves me: because I freely lay down my life. And so I am free to take it up again. No one takes it from me. I lay it down of my own free will. I have the right to lay it down; I also have the right to take it up again. I received this authority personally from my Father."

I love this passage and believe the words shed significant light on the problem(s) of loneliness. The Shepherd's (Jesus') intent and desire is for the sheep to be seen, to be valued, to be known, and to be safe. The Shepherd makes sure of this by his actions of care and sacrifice. This isn't the intent of the "sheep rustler" (Satan), however. His main objective is to cause confusion, create fear, and become a distraction from the Shepherd's voice. Let me pose it as a question: What if the main point of confusion for the sheep rustler is making the sheep lonely? The Shepherd's promise is life—and life to the fullest. It only makes sense that the sheep rustler's purpose is to steal, kill, and destroy. Loneliness is the perfect weapon.

Part I has focused on the problem(s) with our culture and the deleterious and confounding effects of loneliness. Part II will explore God's original intent and design. We'll explore Scripture as well as the biology and spirituality of relationships, fellowship, connection, and belonging. Finally, Part III will provide a practical and tangible framework for individuals, families, and faith communities to combat and eradicate the loneliness epidemic.

Questions for Reflection

1. What's your definition of success? How has this definition helped you? How has it hindered you?

2. How have you seen screens and social media affect you or your family? What have been the effects?

3. Have you ever intentionally or unintentionally joined a tribe? What was the situation? What drew you to the tribe? What was the result?

4. How can you adjust your life or family rhythms (use of screens, solitude versus community, and so on) to nurture more flourishing for you and the people you care most about?

Part II

GOD'S DESIGN

4

THE ORIGINAL DESIGN

Coming Back into Alignment

Loneliness, I am pretty sure, is one of the ways by which we can grow
spiritually. Until we are lonely we may easily think we have got further
than we really have in Christian love; our (natural and innocent, but
merely natural, not heavenly) pleasure in being loved—in being, as you say,
an object of interest to someone—can be mistaken for progress in love itself,
the outgoing active love which is concerned with giving, not receiving.
It is this latter which is the beginning of sanctity.

C. S. LEWIS

I DON'T KNOW ABOUT YOU, but I tend to analyze and pick apart everything. I know it drives my wife, Sarah, crazy at times, but before I decide on something, I want to make sure that I have all the information. As Sarah says, I can talk things to death. This can be a good thing, but it can also be a bad thing.

I started to question why I do this. One glaringly obvious reason is that I want to make sure that I don't do anything wrong, don't want to make a bad decision or enter a problem that I can't fix. I think that this is typical for humans; we can be so focused on a problem that we lose sight of everything else around us. In my attempt to avoid the problem, I become hyperfocused on it. This produces a glass-half-empty mindset that can significantly distort reality.

In some ways, this is what Part I of this book feels like. If we stayed focused on Part I and the problems it describes, we would maintain a pretty dismal mindset. Furthermore, many of us don't need a whole lot of help identifying or being reminded of the problem because it is squarely in front of our faces. What many of us need help with is seeing the bigger picture—being gently reminded of how God intended relationship and connection to be and then stepping into the original promises of God.

Original Intent

Being a counselor is a job that I don't take lightly. Sitting with clients' stories, in the innermost, vulnerable places of their lives, is a sacred honor. I'm constantly humbled that so many people have entrusted me with their stories. Over the past ten-plus years of being a counselor, I've come to realize that many people are acutely aware of their problem but are lost when it comes to a solution. My job as a counselor is to walk alongside my clients in their journey toward health and remind them of the way God designed and intended things to be.

For my youth ministry and biblical studies degree, I was required to learn biblical Greek and Hebrew—an arduous task, but it was worthwhile to learn how to study the original languages of Scripture. Our modern translations are good, but they miss out on the depth and richness of the authors' original intent. For example, there are multiple meanings for love in the New Testament. If we took the English word at face value, we'd miss out on the depth, complexity, and meaning of the original Greek.

A desire to search for deeper meaning and understanding moved me to explore the original language of Genesis 1–2. What

I found helped me understand more clearly God's original design for his creation.

At face value in English, Genesis 2:7—"GOD formed man out of dirt from the ground and blew into his nostrils the breath of life. The Man came alive—a living soul!"—is a nice, comforting story of how humankind was created. But if you dig deeper below the surface of the English language, the richness of the original language will blow your mind.

- *"GOD formed man."* The word *formed* is the Greek action verb *plasso*, which means to form, to shape, or to mold. If I close my eyes and try to imagine what this looks like, I see an artist painting in detail, a potter gently working clay, or a sculptor meticulously manipulating stone with a chisel and a hammer. This act of forming or shaping didn't just happen; it took intention. In fact, it was different from the previous days of creation, when God made or spoke things into existence. In Genesis 1, God made (*poieo*) and God spoke or commanded (*epo*) things into existence, which is categorically different from forming or shaping (*plasso*). These differences show the intentional value God desired when he designed us.

- *"Blew into his nostrils the breath of life."* Think about the positioning here for a minute. God, the triune God (Father–Son–Holy Spirit), had just finished crafting, molding, forming, and shaping his creation, and it was time to bring that creation alive. He didn't decide to just prop up Adam and move him along, nor did he just "speak" or "command" Adam to life, like he did with the rest of creation. What he did do was look Adam in the face and breathe (*emphusao*) life (*zōē*) into him. This intentional action of breathing shows the transfer of both physical and spiritual life from God to humankind. What takes this to the next level of amazing is that the word for life (*zōē*) is different from the word for life in Genesis 1: *zōon*, or living creature.

- *"The man came alive—a living soul!"* There was one more step in the process of creating humankind, something that distinguishes us from the rest of creation. Part of breathing life is that we not only come alive physically, but we come alive spiritually, as well. *Psuche*, or soul, is the vital breath of life; the human soul is the direct aftermath of God breathing into Adam!

I'm not sure if you feel the same way I did after reading this, but it blew me away. I had to pause and take it all in. To borrow phrasing from television infomercials: "But wait—there's more!" We weren't just created, formed, shaped, or molded after any random thing; we were created in the image of the triune God. Genesis 1:26-27 states:

- *"God spoke: 'Let us make human beings in our image, make them reflecting our nature'* . . . *God created human beings; he created them godlike, reflecting God's nature. He created them male and female."* Being made in the image (*eikon*) of the triune God indicates a mirror-like representation. It, in effect, assumes a prototype of which it's not merely a resemblance but an exact model from which it is drawn, molded, created, or formed. We reflect (*homoiosis*) the nature of the triune God, which means that we are similar in likeness, appearance, resemblance, or identity to our Creator.

If this information hasn't affected you or caused you to pause, go back and read it again! The triune God intentionally chose to meticulously mold us into God's image and likeness, then breathe life into us and impart tangible aspects of God's self into us. WOW!

To be honest, I had to stop researching several times to wipe away tears. The God of the universe willingly chose to slow down and take the time to create you and me as his crowning masterpiece. Intimate understanding of our creation does two things. First, it illuminates the reason why the evil one would want to destroy the very fabric of this original intent through loneliness. Second, it creates a framework for us to begin exploring God's original design for connection, community, attachment, and relationship.

What I want us to consider in this moment is: Why did the triune God design it this way? Why did he create the heavens and the earth and everything in them? Was it for his pleasure? Then why did he create humankind? He doesn't need us, but he wanted to step into fellowship and relationship with his creation, so he created Adam. I find it fascinating that he didn't stop there. Yes, Adam was created in the image of God, but it wasn't good for Adam to be alone (Genesis 2:18-20), so God created woman to strengthen, complement, and partner man. Through the creation of woman, there was a fuller and more complete reflection of the triune God, manifesting in a deeper, more holistic physical, relational, mental, emotional, and spiritual connection. God's plan from the beginning was connection and relationship. It's encoded in our DNA. Loneliness and isolation are repurposed and perfected lies of the evil one attempting to disrupt and confuse us.

It must be noted that our loneliness isn't solved if we find someone to marry; it isn't even solved if we make a profession of faith and enter a me-and-Jesus relationship. It's solved when we're invited into the family of God, with our messiness and all!

If it's in our DNA that we were meant to engage in perfect relationship with our Creator and others, it would make sense that every part of our being—including the depths of our soul—yearns and longs to return to the original design. Perfection was thwarted in the Fall, and ever since, humans have been desperately searching for reconnection. We must develop an understanding of the way humans were meant to live.

Questions for Reflection

1. How does knowing God's original intention for you and me affect how you see God?

2. Now that you have a deeper understanding of the root of loneliness, how does that make you feel?

3. What does it feel like to know that we reflect all relational aspects of the triune God?

IT WAS MEANT TO BE THIS WAY

How We Are Hardwired for Connection

What defines us as Christians is not most profoundly that we have come to know him but that he took note of us and made us his own.

JOHN PIPER

Any man could, if he were so inclined, be the sculptor of his own brain.

SANTIAGO RAMÓN Y CAJAL

ONE OF MY GREATEST PRIVILEGES during high school was being a caregiver to my grandparents on my mom's side of the family. Nana and Grandad, as we called them, had followed us out from California several years after we moved to Colorado. They bought a sprawling ranch home that backed up to a golf course. The home was large, and the yard was even larger. By the time they moved to Colorado, they were already in their late seventies, moving into their early eighties. Their home took a lot of work, and they needed extra help. I'd head over after school every day to do some yard work. I also helped with tasks around the house, and when my grandad was diagnosed with Parkinson's disease, I helped as an extra caregiver.

My grandad was a very introverted man and often painfully

quiet. Growing up, I was intimidated by his silence and often wondered what he was thinking. I knew my mom had a strained relationship with him when she was growing up, which seemed to improve as she got older. I was determined to ask questions, listen to stories, and get to know my grandad.

Throughout the course of several months, I began to peel back the layers of his life. Listening to story after story, I started to realize he never had a relational foundation to build from when he was young. He grew up in isolation as an only child in Philadelphia. His mom came from money, and his dad was an accountant for a local brewery. They lived in a large mansion on Sherwood Avenue, and he was routinely driven to school by a chauffeur.

After graduating high school, he enrolled at Massachusetts Institute of Technology (MIT), where he pursued an engineering degree. He also maintained a spot on the university gymnastics team. Upon graduating from MIT, he was offered a job with Bell Laboratories and worked there for several years. Then, in 1940, he was offered a job at a start-up company in Palo Alto, California, called Hewlett-Packard (HP). He worked for Hewlett-Packard from 1940 to 1980.

I didn't realize how amazing his HP stories were until Nana asked me to clean and organize the basement bookshelves. I love history, books, and artifacts of time gone by, so what would have taken someone else several hours to clean and organize took me several days. Going through their stuff, I found books on books of graph-lined paper where my grandad had written calculations, formulas, and schematics for projects he'd worked on at HP. These hand-drawn schematics were beautiful works of art. I wish I had one or two of his drawings still, but we ended up donating them to the HP Computer Museum in California. I began asking my grandad questions based on what I had found. His eyes would light up, and his stories would get richer with detail.

On one of my cleaning days, I came across something that stopped me in my tracks. While flipping through an old book, I found a program and certificate for the Army–Navy "Excellence in Production" ("E") Award. Grandad was given this award in the 1940s for his work in developing and supplying audio oscillators to the military. (Their Model 200B audio oscillators were also used for the Disney movie *Fantasia*.) I didn't know what an audio oscillator was, even after he tried to explain it to me, but I thought what he was able to contribute to and accomplish was cool.

When my grandad turned ninety, Bill Hewlett and Dave Packard sent him their most recent computer chip framed next to a computer chip he worked on prior to retiring. He often stopped by that picture as we were walking down the hallway and smiled with pride.

I asked him once to explain the difference between hardware and software. He said *hardware* is the physical device; *software* is what is or can be programmed on the hardware. Hardware cannot be changed or manipulated without ruining the device, whereas software can be reprogrammed or changed. Software needs hardware to function, and hardware doesn't reach its fullest potential without partnering with software. His answer will always stick with me—and it has an interesting correlation to our conversation about loneliness.

Hardware

Have you ever given any thought to how we were designed? Every aspect of who we are was purposely planned out. Psalm 139:13 tells us: "You created my inmost being; you knit me together in my mother's womb" (NIV). This passage shows us that God uniquely designed us for something special. Throughout the Scriptures, we see God's desire for rescue and relationship. We see his desire to connect intimately with us—and his desire for us to connect intimately with others. God intentionally hardwired us for connection.

The way God designed us to operate in this world is quite complex. It astounds me that much of what we know about the brain and the body has only come into existence in the past forty years. The deeper we dive into the molecular structures of the brain and body, the more we realize how complex our systems are. And the more we comprehend the complexity of our systems, the more this knowledge points us to our Creator.

Take the brain, for instance. Did you know that the brain is the only organ/muscle in the body that doesn't have to deteriorate with age? If we intentionally engage our brain, it will strengthen and grow. Here are several mind-blowing facts about the brain:

- Your brain consists of approximately eighty-six billion neurons (brain cells).[1]
- There are anywhere between 1,000 and 100,000 synapse connections for each neuron, averaging about 40,000.[2]
- There are roughly a million gigabytes of storage space in your brain. Most smartphones have less than 256 gigabytes.[3]
- "A piece of brain tissue the size of a grain of sand contains 100,000 neurons and 1 billion synapses, all communicating with each other."[4]
- Information in the brain moves at about 260 miles per hour. This is faster than a Formula 1 race car, which tops out at 231.5 miles per hour.[5]

- "There's a reason the brain has been called a 'random thought generator.' The average brain is believed to generate up to 50,000 thoughts per day."[6]
- Human beings will continue to make new neural connections throughout life in response to mental activity and stimuli.[7]

There are hundreds, if not thousands, more facts like these that speak to the incredible nature of the brain. When I speak to schools, organizations, and churches, and I share this information, an audience member always jokingly states, "All this thinking about my thinking is making my brain hurt!" I'm convinced that the more we know about how the brain works, the better equipped we will be to combat this loneliness epidemic.

Just like the hardware (structural components) of my grandad's designs many years ago, we each have key hardware components in our brain. To simplify the complexities of the brain's inner workings, I'll use the heuristic of 1-2-3-4-5.[8] For every *one* brain, there are *two* hemispheres, *three* levels of functional governance, *four* lobes, and *five* systems of integration.

One Brain: The brain is a complex supercomputer made up of approximately eighty-six billion **neurons** (brain cells). (I don't know about you, but attempting to comprehend eighty-six billion is a difficult task for me.) Interestingly, these eighty-six billion neurons only make up 10 percent of the brain structure; the other 90 percent is made up of insulating cells called **glial cells.** Not much is known about glial cells, but it's speculated that their sole purpose is to insulate, protect, and enhance the functioning of the eighty-six billion neurons.

Two Hemispheres: The one brain is divided into two distinct yet similar parts, the right and left hemispheres. The **left hemisphere** is responsible for literality (facts and details), language (speech and reasoning), linearity (straight-line thinking), and logic (reasoning and analysis). The right hemisphere is the hub of sensory (auditory and visual) input and processing, creativity, and spatial awareness. The two work in tandem. The **right hemisphere** creates pictorial representations of the logic and language from the left hemisphere.[9]

Three Levels of Functional Governance: The easiest way to describe the three levels of functional governance is the hand model. Hold up your hand, like you're getting ready to wave to a friend. The base of the hand, the wrist, and the arm make up your **nervous system**. The base of your hand (palm area) makes up the **hindbrain**. Now, fold your thumb over to touch the middle of your palm, and that becomes the **midbrain**, the part of the brain that engages emotion and our fight-or-flight responses. Finally, close your fingers over your thumb and make a fist. This is the **forebrain** or **cerebral cortex**, the part of the brain that engages in higher-order thinking.

The hindbrain has four distinct functions: The **pons** (linked to sleep and arousal); the **cerebellum** (linked to motor movements); the **medulla** (linked to life functions such as heart beating and breathing); the **reticular formation** (linked to sleep, arousal, and attention). The functions of the hindbrain are vital for life but operate outside the scope of our consciousness.

The midbrain has five distinct functions: The **superior colliculus** (line to visual processing, in tandem with the occipital lobe); the **inferior colliculus** (linked to auditory processing);

the **substantia nigra** (linked to movement); the **ventral tegmental area** (linked to rewarding effects of food, sex, etc.); and the **pineal gland** (linked to daily seasonal rhythms).

The **forebrain** or **cerebral cortex** distinguishes us from the rest of creation as it provides us with higher-order thinking, reasoning, and processing.

Four Lobes: To further break down the brain, we can view it in four lobes. The **frontal lobe**, located at the front part of our head from the forehead around to the front of the ears, is made up of four structures: the **precentral gyrus** (which controls the motor cortex and motor functions); the **secondary motor cortex** (which plans movement with the basal ganglia); **Broca's area** (which is in charge of speech and language production); and the **prefrontal cortex** (which guides and controls abstract thought, reasoning, planning, working memory, and conscious sensations).

Located on either side of the brain just behind the ears, the **temporal lobe** is responsible for processing memories, sounds, and smells and forming memories.

Immediately behind the frontal lobe and above the temporal lobes is the **parietal lobe**, which controls and responds to touch-related information (e.g., temperature, pressure, and pain). The parietal lobe also contains the **somatosensory cortex**, which is responsible for touch sensation; detecting body movements and positions; and **Wernicke's area**, which enables language comprehension.

Finally, located at the back of the head, the **occipital lobe** is in charge of vision and visual recognition.

Five Systems: The last component of the 1-2-3-4-5 heuristic is the five systems that interact with the brain: the **central, peripheral, autonomic, sympathetic,** and **parasympathetic nervous systems.**

The brain and spinal column make up the **central nervous system,** which relays messages and information to muscles and organs from the brain and then back to the brain from those same muscles and organs.

The **peripheral nervous system** is made up of the **somatic** and **autonomic nervous systems.** The **somatic nervous system** is in charge of communicating with motor neurons, whose purpose is to stimulate muscles around our skeletal system. The **autonomic nervous system** works with smooth muscles such as the heart, stomach, other organs, and blood vessels.

The **autonomic nervous system** manages the body's flight-or-fight response (stress response). It's divided into two systems, the **sympathetic nervous system** and the **parasympathetic system.**

The **sympathetic nervous system** is our protector; it jumps into action when there's a perceived or real threat. To do this, it activates multiple systems such as increasing heart rate, dilating pupils, slowing or stopping digestion, stimulating adrenal glands, and constricting blood vessels. Simply put: The sympathetic nervous system is meant to keep us out of danger and alive.

The job of the **parasympathetic nervous system** is to bring the body back to equilibrium after the sympathetic nervous system is activated. The parasympathetic nervous system brings homeostasis by slowing heart rate, constricting pupils, resuming digestion, restricting adrenal gland secretion, and returning breathing to normal.

Congratulations! You've just had a crash course in brain science. I promise you there's a reason for this exploration of our neural biology! How we connect and engage in relationships is correlatively connected to our brain's health and development. The hardware can be affected by the software.

Software
Hardware can't change, but its capacity and potential are linked to software. The programmable components of the hardware are directly linked to and affected by the type and quality of the software. It is common knowledge in the counseling world that early childhood development is crucial to the health and development of the brain. For the most part, all of us are born with the same hardware, but the software differs based on how we're nurtured.

To explore the important symbiotic relationship between hardware and software components of the brain, let me introduce you to Jon.

My experience as an in-home family therapist is one that I'll never forget. I only lasted nine difficult, unforgettable months. Jon was assigned to me during the middle of his sophomore year of high school. His parents were concerned about his explosive behavior toward peers and teachers. His last outburst had gotten him expelled from school. He had been required to do online school from home, which had been a disaster. By the time I entered the picture, the police had been called over a dozen times. After the last call, he was facing charges for choking a neighbor kid.

Jon was on house arrest and could not venture outside his

single-wide mobile home. I would go to the house, ask the parents to step outside, and do my best to conduct some semblance of therapy. As you can imagine, we didn't get very far. One day, I decided I was going to challenge Jon and not let up until I got some sort of reaction from him. So I confronted him on his behavior toward his parents. I pushed until I started to get an emotional reaction, then something surprising happened. Jon completely broke. He lunged across the room and started to choke me. His dad, who was just outside, heard the commotion, rushed inside, and pulled him off me. I was shaken up, but I'd noticed something as Jon was coming toward me. There was little-to-no spark of life in his eyes. That bothered me more than getting choked, and I was determined to figure out what was going on. I thought it was biological rather than behavioral.

After a long fight with his psychiatrist (which almost cost me my job), I was able to convince them to run some extra tests. One of the tests was a sleep-deprived EEG; the other was a neurotransmitter screening. The results were astonishing. First, the EEG detected multiple small frontal-cortex seizures that would throw him into fight-or-flight mode; second, he was highly deficient in GABA, a neurotransmitter that helps calm us down after an emotional upset. What would happen is that Jon would "black out" or lose consciousness briefly with the seizures then would come to and be thrown into a fight-or-flight response. This would then cause him to react by lunging at anyone or anything around him. Furthermore, because of his low GABA levels, Jon couldn't return to proper homeostasis.

As frightening as it was to be on the receiving end of one of Jon's outbursts, I could only imagine how frightening it was for him to be out of control. The doctors put him on an anti-seizure medication and a GABA supplement, and within a matter of weeks, he became the kind, calm, intelligent, and respectful kid his parents once knew.

We already considered that we're hardwired by God for connection and relationships with others as a reflection of the triune nature of God. Our brains are designed toward this type of connection. We also considered that due to the original sin that separated us from God, our created nature has been corrupted, and as a result, we chase this primordial longing through meaningless and trivial pursuits. We require healing in the deepest parts of us. As we'll discover, the only thing that can truly fill the void is a saving relationship with Jesus Christ.

In the next chapter, we'll explore the power of attachment bonds, both developmentally (e.g., our critical growth milestones) and situationally as we develop in our relationships. We'll also unpack the power of our own presence.

Questions for Reflection

1. What was your biggest "aha moment" from this chapter?

2. What does it feel like to know that our brains are always able to grow and change?

3. How does the idea that we're hardwired for connection and relationship affect how you see God and others?

6

THE DEEP LONGING

The Importance of Attachment

*A sum can be put right: but only by going back till you find the error
and working it afresh from that point, never by simply going on.*

C. S. LEWIS

SEVERAL YEARS AGO, my wife and I were in a heated exchange.
Okay, I'll admit—it was a full-blown argument. I can't remember
what we were arguing about, but I do remember how I made her
feel. In my attempt to defend my position, I completely dismissed
what she was trying to express. In a moment of deep hurt and
frustration, she blurted out, "Why can't you just listen?"

I don't remember how I responded to that. In all honesty, I
probably thought I *was* listening, hearing words. But I was completely missing the point. I was listening to respond, not listening
to hear her heart. My actions isolated her and most likely created a
disconnect between us. If I had left it there, that disconnect could
have developed into a rift of loneliness, which could've complicated

our marriage. She longed for me to see what she really needed, to connect with her to validate why she was hurting and frustrated. If I had known to hear with understanding, beyond the words, I could have created a safe place for her to be vulnerable and loved, thus making our connection healthier and stronger.

The deepest desire of every human being is to be seen, valued, and loved—to be securely attached to another human being despite our shortcomings, faults, struggles, and inconsistencies. To many of us, this type of connection seems idyllic and unrealistic. We've struggled with disconnect, hurt, anxiety, depression. Our own relational models growing up were distorted, and we don't have the tools, resources, or even the right direction to achieve what our heart wants. The desire for secure attachment is there, but the path forward is clouded with fear and distrust. In many ways, this is why loneliness is so insidious: We recognize what we're missing but don't have a plan to fill that void. In this chapter, I'll provide you with the substantive materials, and in Part III, I'll share a plan and the tools to build (or rebuild) secure attachment.

A client whose world was falling apart around him couldn't nail down why. By pure chance, one of his friends had my card and encouraged him to call me. After several months, and as a last resort, he ended up giving me a call. I won't forget our first meeting. He walked into my office and threw himself on my couch, slumping like an irritated teenager. I quickly glanced at my intake paperwork to make sure I had his age right. He was a thirty-six-year-old man acting like a fourteen-year-old boy.

Counselors are trained to observe and explore without bias or judgment, so I sat back and allowed the process to happen. Week after week, he'd come in and throw himself down on my couch. He'd engage in conversation, but he often gave short responses that were dripping with sarcasm and disdain. I was able to determine that he was in the midst of a breakup, he was on probation for caustic behavior at work, and his friends were actively avoiding him. In all honesty, after eight sessions, I was beginning to understand how his friends felt.

In the ninth session, instead of letting him continue down this path, I confronted him: "Man! No wonder your friends are avoiding you. If you're treating them the same way you're treating me in here, I would avoid you too! It almost makes me think you're doing it on purpose."

He immediately sat up (for the first time in nine sessions), looked at me in the eye (also the first time in nine sessions), and just stared at me. I held his gaze. It slowly softened from piercing anger to sadness. He began weeping—not with the kind of tear that trickles down your face when you watch a sappy commercial but full-on losing it. I gave the space for him to cry. When he was able to look up, he stated, "I don't know what to do. I need help."

I reflected out loud that it seemed like he was trying his best to push people away because he was afraid of vulnerability, but I didn't know how to change that way of thinking. Over the next several sessions, he revealed that his dad had been a workaholic businessman and that his mom, unable to cope with being a "single" parent, would escape with large amounts of alcohol. I realized he hadn't had a secure attachment model growing up. As a result, he struggled to attach to others. When people tried to get close, he'd retreat or avoid, pushing them away.

One comment he made stuck with me: "Doc, it's not that I don't *want* to be close to people. I just don't know how to." He knew his current functioning wasn't ideal (or even what he wanted), but it was all he knew. Once he verbalized his past, and as we collaboratively developed a plan, he was able to reclaim what was lost and to begin healing. He made and maintained a healthy, trusting relationship with a new girlfriend, and two years after he completed counseling, I was invited to his wedding!

What Is Attachment, and Why Is It So Important?

Attachment is—if not *the* most important and fundamental aspect—a bedrock of relationship. Our attachment models are typically developed in unconscious interactions with our primary caregivers between birth and three years old. Practically, this means that as a preverbal child, our relational interactions have a deep fundamental impact on our attachment and the blueprint for future relationships. I'll first discuss the way attachment was intended to be and then what can happen in a world marred by sin.

Oxytocin is a hormone released when we're in an intimate relationship with someone. It's often referred to as the "cuddle" hormone and has imprinting qualities. This means that when this hormone is released, it increases the connectedness of those involved. If there's true mutual intimacy and trust during intercourse, release of oxytocin deepens and enhances the couple's attachment to one another.

Oxytocin is also released during a vaginal birth and transferred between mother and child. This natural transmission sets the stage for healthy attachment between them. And oxytocin is released during the initial days of life as the baby experiences skin-on-skin contact with his or her mother or father. These initial interactions with the caregiver(s) lay the foundation for secure attachment in the future. This means that the baby knows his or her caregiver is a secure base. Early on, this is an intrinsic, unconscious understanding, but as the child grows, it becomes a cognitive and verbal understanding: *Mom and dad are safe. Therefore, I can venture out into the world, try new things, develop relationships, and explore, knowing that I always have someone safe to come back to.*

As I studied attachment early on in my counseling career, I became deeply frustrated with the divide between what it was supposed to look like and what it was actually like. At times, it was quite depressing. Yet as I continued to study, I began to realize just how many things could be redeemed. Disconnection and detachment are not permanent!

How is this accomplished? To reach a solution, we must first understand the fundamentals of attachment. The easiest framework for understanding secure attachment comes from author, psychiatrist, and neuroscientist Dr. Daniel Siegel. Siegel states that in order to develop a secure attachment, you must have three components: You need to feel seen, safe, and soothed.[1]

Are you seen? Often when I'm speaking at an organization, school, or place of faith, I ask, "When was the last time you were seen?" Typically, the response is "I was seen yesterday by _____ (insert name)." When I press a bit, I'm told that being "seen" means having someone say hi in passing, exchange pleasantries, and then part ways with you. This isn't being seen; this is being noticed, at best. Truly *seeing* someone means holding their gaze as they're talking and engaging with their inner world. Seeing is moving past the pleasantries and stepping into real life, moving from "Hi, how are you today?" and "I'm fine." to "No, really, how are you doing? I know you've had a hard week. How are you holding up?" and creating a safe space for an honest response.

The key to seeing others is being curious and persistent. The key to being seen is risking being vulnerable. When we truly see or are truly seen, a piece of us is redeemed and a broken part begins to heal.

Are you safe? Can you effectively connect relationally with someone when you don't feel safe with them? The answer is absolutely not!

Safety is twofold. You must be safe physically, meaning safe from harm and physically cared for—having a roof over your head and a place to lay your head at night, knowing where your next meal is coming from. And you need emotional and psychological safety. Put simply, does the person you are attempting to attach with feel relationally dangerous?

When I was working in the jail-diversion program early on in my career, I held "reunification" sessions for adolescents getting out of detention or a halfway house and their parents. I vividly remember one session when a dad was quite livid with his son. During the session, he turned toward me and snarled, "Why is my son doing this? I can't believe his behavior! He has a roof over his head, a place to sleep, and food to eat . . . I don't get it."

Unphased by his anger, I spent the next twenty minutes affirming the dad as a good provider . . . and explaining that he needed to take it one step further because his son was emotionally and psychologically scared of him. I'm not sure what happened in that moment, but something clicked in the dad's mind. He started to cry, which freaked out his son, who had never seen his dad cry. The dad went on to share that his own dad had been an abusive drunk. He honestly believed he was a good dad because he at least wasn't hitting his kids.

With this breakthrough and over the next fifteen sessions, I helped father and son reconnect, heal past wounds, and develop a foundation of physical, emotional, and psychological safety. If the family had been of faith, I would've helped lay a foundation of spiritual safety, as well. (I'll break down how to do this practically in later chapters.)

Are you soothed? This final concept is important yet very simple. To answer this question, ask yourself whether you feel better after being with your caregiver than you did before you spent time with them.

I love my daughters. Being a dad is one of the best things on this planet! Raising two daughters is a blessing and a challenge. As they grow, they experience new emotions and feelings, some of which are overwhelming. When one of my daughters is upset, I can take one of two approaches.

I can take my perspective as a male in his late thirties and tell them their emotions don't line up with their circumstances. I can try convincing them that it's not that big of a deal and tell them to get over it. Problem solved—or is it? They might stop emoting, but they've received no soothing from me. I told them to suck it up. Chances are, the next time they're upset, they won't let me know.

Or I can focus on them. I can get down on their level and do my best to understand their perspective of the event. I can sit with them in the emotion, attempt to understand why they're upset, and allow them to emote. It's like Sadness and Bing Bong in the Disney/Pixar movie *Inside Out*.[2] Bing Bong, Riley's imaginary friend, is coming to grips with the fact that the need for his existence is dwindling. Joy, wanting to keep things upbeat, pressures Bing Bong to be happy. Her well-intentioned, upbeat attitude dismisses Bing Bong's experience. At one point in the movie, Bing Bong sits down and begins to cry. Joy tries to move him along, but Sadness sits down next to him, validates him, allows him to cry, and hugs him. Within moments, Bing Bong looks up and says that he feels better now. This is such a beautiful picture of being soothed. Practically, being soothed is not being fixed but rather being validated, heard, and sat with. (This can look different for everyone.)

Being Seen

I love working with horses. There's something about a horse that creates a mixture of awe, wonder, fear, joy, and safety. When I was struggling in middle school and high school, my horse and other horses at the barn were my safe and calm place. I'll be honest; I didn't fully comprehend the therapeutic and relational power of horses until I became a counselor.

One of my jobs at the community mental health center was to develop an equine-facilitated therapy program. We partnered with a barn in eastern Colorado Springs and began taking kids there to work with horses. There wasn't any riding involved; rather, the kids learned to connect with, care for, and lead the horses from the ground. If you know anything about horses, you know that they're prey animals. This means that they're hypersensitive to anything that could potentially bring them harm. For example, if a kid walked up to the horse with his hands behind his back, the horse would be resistant and unwilling to engage with him, for fear of the unknown (i.e., what's behind the back). The dynamic of horses as prey animals was a powerful tool for the therapy session. It forced the kids to be present in the moment and congruent with their feelings.

Let me introduce you to Clay and the first time he was truly seen. Clay, an eleven-year-old who struggled with emotional regulation, was referred to the program by his therapist. His emotional outbursts at school were becoming a consistent pattern, and he was close to getting expelled. Home was not much better; his mom and grandfather reported extreme tantrums that resulted in damaged property. Clay's therapist felt that Clay could benefit from being outside and working with horses.

I was surprised when I first met Clay. From reading his file, I expected a rough kid with a defiant attitude and a big temper. Instead, Clay was a small, wiry kid who was short for his age. His energy and curiosity caused him to fidget constantly. He also had a condition that caused his calf muscles to overly tighten, which caused him to walk, unbalanced, on his toes.

Clay was so excited to be at the ranch. To ensure his safety, he was paired with me as his guide and given the most docile horse to work with. This horse was very similar in personality to Eeyore in the Winnie-the-Pooh stories. It seemed like not much would faze this horse. But for some reason, the energy that Clay brought to the session was so intense that his horse wanted nothing to do with him and did everything she could to avoid him. I quickly recognized Clay was getting frustrated while trying to groom the horse. I stopped Clay and asked him to take a step back. "Clay, I want you to try something for me."

"WHAT?" he responded with disdain in his voice.

"I want you to take a moment to focus on your breathing and calm down," I replied.

"Well, how do I do that?" he quipped.

"Close your eyes. Take a deep breath in through your nose, allowing your lungs to expand fully. Hold it for 4-3-2-1-0, and then blow out through your mouth until all your breath is pushed out."

Reluctantly, Clay started the breathing exercise. I asked him to take a step closer to his horse. "Now keep your eyes closed and continue focusing on your breathing. Put your hands up and continue breathing." As Clay was doing this grounding exercise, I kept an eye on his horse and noticed she, too, was calming down.

Several moments later, a beautiful collision happened! As Clay was continuing to breathe with his hands up, his horse took a deep breath and leaned into his hands. Getting a handful of the horse's mane, Clay abruptly opened his eyes and looked at me. "Breathe," I said. "Just continue to breathe." For ten minutes, Clay stood there regulating his breath while being seen by and connected to his horse.

From that point on, when Clay arrived at the barn, he'd get out of the car, rush to the front of the barn, do his ten to fifteen sets of mindful breathing, then connect with his horse. Several weeks later, his grandfather pulled me aside and conveyed that Clay was respectful at home, engaging with his family, and improving at school. There were no more outbursts, and his grades were improving. In fact, he told me that when Clay got upset at home, he'd stop and breathe. There was life-changing power in Clay's connection to his horse.

Quantum Physics and the Power of Presence

Understanding the importance of attachment bonds is a critical step in the process of fully realizing God's design and intent for our lives. Being seen, safe, and soothed are key components in this formula, but if we just stopped there, we'd be stopping significantly short of the goal. There is greater, intended power in our presence, more than many of us realize.

To fully understand the importance and power of presence, we must look at the emerging field of quantum physics. Traditional physics is the study of matter and its motion through space and time. A traditional, or Newtonian, physicist will study anything that has mass and volume, focusing on the interplay of its energy and force on time and space. Simply put: A physicist studies how matter interacts with other matter in our physical world.

I was never good at math, and so I never reached the physics course in high school or college. As a counselor watching clients' body language and facial features, I began questioning the reality of only the physical. I acutely listened to the words that were coming out of their mouths, but they always put off a unique, distinct energy in our sessions. I was determined to figure out what was happening. In my research, I stumbled across the concept of quantum physics.

For centuries, atoms were thought to be the smallest building blocks of science. But further research has revealed smaller particles like protons, neutrons, and electrons. Quantum physics provides a detailed explanation of how atoms work. Furthermore, quantum theory has helped describe and expand our understanding of photons—particles in electromagnetic waves that are even smaller than electrons, protons, and neutrons. Light sources such as a candle or laser emit photons. The more photons a laser shoots off, the brighter the light.[3]

To better comprehend quantum physics, we need a basic understanding of wavelengths. Light is a form of energy that behaves like a wave in the ocean. The space between the top of one wave and the top of an adjacent wave is called a wavelength. Each photon package carries a certain amount of energy (quantum) depending on its wavelength. The height of a wavelength (as measured from the top of the peak to the bottom of the trough) is called its amplitude. The number of wave peaks per second, also known as hertz (Hz), is referred to as its frequency. The longer the wavelength, the lower the frequency. The shorter the wavelength, the higher the frequency.[4] Some types of wavelengths:

> *Light waves:* There are many wavelengths that we can't see; however, there's a visible electromagnetic spectrum that we can see. This spectrum encompasses all the electromagnetic radiation that occurs in the world, including gamma rays, X-rays, ultraviolet light, visible light, infrared rays, microwaves, and radio waves. For humans, the visible-light spectrum is very narrow, between approximately 380 and 740 nanometers. Our perception of color is associated with wavelengths. Red is

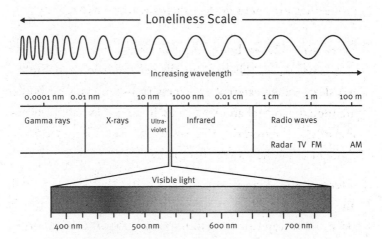

associated with longer wavelengths, while blues and violets are associated with shorter wavelengths (see Figure 4).

Sound waves: Sound waves have similar characteristics to light waves. The frequency or wavelength of the sound is associated with our perception of its pitch. High-frequency sound waves are perceived as high-pitched sounds, while low-frequency sound waves are perceived as low-pitch sounds.

The brain produces waves by synchronized electrical pulses from the communication of neurons. Brain waves are measured by placing sensors on predetermined places on the scalp. Each type of brain wave has its own frequency, from slow to fast. Our brain waves change with what we are thinking, doing, or feeling, so our mind, relationships, and environment can play a role in brain wave frequency and health.

Here are the different types of brain waves, with a short description of each. Please note that this is a basic description—brain waves are far more complex than these descriptions suggest.

Delta waves: Delta brain waves are slow, low frequency, or long wavelengths. They're typically generated in deep, dreamless sleep, where external awareness is suspended. Our bodies are thought to heal and regenerate in delta-wave sleep, which makes deep, restorative sleep essential. Delta waves are also thought to be the source of empathy.

Theta waves: Theta waves have a slightly shorter wavelength and are most present in sleep. When we're in a theta state of sleep, we're typically dreaming vividly beyond our normal

-10

conscious awareness. Theta waves are linked to learning, memory, and intuition.

Alpha waves: Alpha waves have an even shorter wavelength and are present during our meditative thinking. Alpha states are typically linked to the here-and-now grounding of the present moment and help with mental calmness and learning.

Beta waves: Our dominant waves, beta waves, are present in our awake states of conscious awareness. With a higher frequency, beta waves keep us present, alert, engaged, and attentive in problem solving and decision making.

Gamma waves: Gamma waves are the fastest brain waves or the waves with the highest frequency and shortest wavelength. Gamma waves are the conductors, processing information from all aspects of the brain without our conscious detection.

I wanted to walk you through this logical development of wavelengths, frequency, and quantum energy to pose this question: *What if we have emotional frequency that produces physical quantum energy that can be passed from one person to another? What if the emotional frequency around us has the power of life or death?* As we've discussed throughout this book, we've been designed in the image of the triune God. This means that we reflect all aspects of who he is. It wouldn't be too far of a logical leap to assume that we're also connected to each other at a subatomic, quantum level.

When I speak to students, parents, teachers, clergy, and the broader community, I illustrate this point by using a sci-fi tube, a clear plastic tube with electrical connections that make it light up and make noise. By itself, a biotube is useless. If I pick it up with one hand, it's still useless. But if I grab one end with my left hand and the other end with my right hand, that completes the circuit, and the biotube lights up and makes noise. To take it a step further, I then ask for a volunteer from the audience to come up and grab one end of the tube while I hold on to the other end. As you might have guessed, nothing happens with the tube until I grab the hand of the person, thus completing the circuit. "Magically," the biotube lights up and makes noise. Finally, to drive home this point of connection and relationship, I ask the audience if we could complete the circuit with everyone in the room. Most of the audience is skeptical, so I have them stand up and connect hands. I then take the biotube and have the person next to me grab the other. And with bated breath, we wait to see if it lights up. Sure enough, it does! Everyone typically cheers with excitement and disbelief. I explain that we're uniquely designed and created to be connected on a mental, emotional, physical, and biological level.

Power of Presence

Have you ever been affected by the mood in your home? I can remember numerous occasions when I came home after an amazing day at work. Clients had had breakthroughs, I was connected to the Holy Spirit, and life was good! Sarah, on the other hand, had had a rough day with the girls and was frustrated, angry, and slightly depressed. All too quickly, my mood would drop to match theirs. It wasn't their fault; it just happened. But their expressed mood affected the mood and energy of our home—and as a result, affected my mood and energy as well. Our presence has power.

Our presence has power in a positive way as well. I met Ruth two weeks after I started my new job at a local community mental health center in Colorado Springs. Sarah and I had just moved our family from Denver in pursuit of a new job. For the previous two years, I'd worked with youth in the juvenile justice system, and so I wasn't used to working with anyone younger than twelve. Ruth was six.

Due to Ruth's specific behavioral struggles, she couldn't come to the office for her counseling appointment, so I went to her home instead. Being an in-home family counselor has its challenges and its perks. One of the perks is the ability to experience the client and family in their own unique environment. I found out quickly that Ruth was going to be a challenging case. Her mom was in jail for drug possession and distribution, and Ruth had been living with her grandparents for about six months. The results had been catastrophic.

I was called to support the grandparents in developing and executing a parenting plan. This collaborative plan would be established for Ruth's grandparents to engage in communication, conflict resolution, boundary development, and discipline (e.g., consequence and reward) practices with her. The only problem was that Ruth wasn't talking at all. Not only was this problematic, but we weren't even sure if she could comprehend what was being said. Her behaviors were explosive and damaging to her surroundings. She never intentionally hurt anyone, but she left a wake of destruction wherever she went. I had no idea how I was going to do therapy with her.

After speaking with my supervisor, we decided to attempt to bring Ruth to the office at a time that wasn't too crowded with other patients. She would come up the back stairs and meet me in front of the play therapy room. Our play therapy room was spectacular. At its center was a sand-tray table that stood four feet off the ground and was five feet by five feet. Around the sand-tray table were rows and rows of shelves with every type of toy, figurine, caricature, tree, house, et cetera. All the toys were placed at eye level for Ruth. The idea for the room was to provide a place for unobstructed play to happen. This would allow me the opportunity to step back and observe.

During our first session, nothing happened. Ruth sat in the corner with her knees to her chest and her arms wrapped around them. So I, too, sat on the floor with my arms wrapped around my knees. Conveying the results of the first session to her grandmother, I found out the deeper story. "When the police found her," the grandmother stated, "she was in the home all by herself. There was a pack 'n play, a bottle, and some crackers. She was still wearing a diaper and was in the room with several malnourished dogs." With tears in her eyes, Ruth's grandmother added, "We don't know how long she was like this, but we are glad she is with us now." This added pertinent information and helped me grasp the gravity of Ruth's story and the fact that she probably didn't know how to play.

Over the course of the next several sessions in the play therapy room, I demonstrated how to use the sand tray by grabbing several figures and placing them into the sand in a representative scene. Each week, she sat in the corner and stared at me. Finally, in the fifth session, something shifted. Ruth entered the room and cleared out every shelf that was on her level and piled the contents on the sand-tray table. She then sat in the same corner and stared at the table. This went on for weeks and weeks. Trusting the process, I didn't intervene or say anything.

In session twenty, something shifted again. Ruth only cleared out one shelf and put those toys on the table. Instead of sitting on the floor, she began to make scenes with the figures. Then, in session twenty-six, something truly miraculous happened. Ruth walked into the room, smiled at me, and walked over to the shelf. She grabbed a house, some human figures, a couple of animals, and a fence or two. She walked over to the table, placed the house in the middle, built the fence around it, and then turned toward me and said, "You want to play?"

Those four simple words ruined me. Do you want to play? "Yes! Let's play!" I said, trying not to cry. I always tell my counseling students that it's okay to show emotion in session but not to cry harder than your client. At that moment, I was doing my best to keep my emotions in check and enjoy the moment. Ruth finally spoke, and what she wanted was to play! We turned a major corner that day. Her behavior at home changed: According to her grandmother, Ruth became very talkative.

Processing this client with my supervisor, I was flabbergasted as to what unfolded. I didn't do a whole lot. I didn't use a theory or technique—all I did was create space for Ruth. My supervisor reminded me that having a consistent and safe place was all she needed, and my kind, gentle, and consistent presence was what allowed the change to happen.

There's so much power in our presence. My consistency, experience, and care with Ruth changed her from the inside out. If you think about this for a moment, it should cause you to pause at the sheer responsibility and power our presence brings.

As we wrap up this section on God's original design, I want to give one last example: mirror neurons. Mirror neurons were discovered in the 1990s by happenstance. Researchers were studying the brains of monkeys and whether the same brain region was affected similarly if the monkey was eating a banana as if it was just looking at a banana. Researchers monitored the neurons firing in the monkey eating the banana and in the other monkeys in the room. The same neurons were being fired in the monkey eating the banana as in the monkeys simply watching the banana being eaten. Further testing these findings, researchers found that this same phenomenon happened in human participants' emotional reactivity. Essentially, if a parent is upset and being expressive or demonstrative in their emotion, the same neurons are firing in the child, who mirrors the emotional reactivity of their parent.

This can also be used as a positive tool. When our kids were small, Sarah read some of my research on mirror neurons. When the girls would get upset or react to life as kids do, she'd cuddle the girls and take deep breaths. Eventually the girls would mirror her actions and calm down as well. She was able to teach our ten-month-old to stop and take deep breaths when she got upset. Now, at almost seven and twelve years old, our girls still mirror Sarah's calm actions and have created their own habits of self-calming. If a child is upset, the mentally and emotionally aware parent can step in with a grounded calmness that helps engage the child's neurons, thus helping them calm down. There is power in our presence.

Bringing It Together

We've covered a lot of information in this chapter and section. It's important for you to know that there's a complexity to how we are designed that we may not fully understand until we get to heaven. What's evident is that *God desires for us to be connected.* He intentionally designed us this way.

Loneliness is most prevalent when there's an absence of connection or attachment. In the world we live in, finding and developing a secure attachment can feel like an impossible task. Moreover, many never had the opportunity or privilege of a secure attachment in childhood and don't have an effective model to replicate. Even if all seems hopeless, there's hope, and the past can be redeemed.

I want you to sit with this for a moment: Every aspect of who we are is designed for connection—mentally, emotionally, physically, and spiritually. If any one of these components is hindered, damaged, or missing, it can have a ripple effect on the entire system. We've talked about the problems of loneliness, and we've talked about God's original design. In Part III, we'll explore how to bring reconciliation and redemption to what we lost in the Fall. I'll discuss practical steps for us to take as individuals, what our personal responsibility is to those around us, and what our communal responsibility is as the body of Christ.

Part III will be a challenge, but I implore you to read it with an honest, vulnerable, teachable, and reflective spirit. Reflect on what needs to change in how you interact with yourself and those around you. There are several steps that must take place for this to happen.

- There needs to be an awareness that something is not okay.
- You must admit the past hurts and is complicated.
- You must be willing to dive into hard things so that healing and redemption can come.
- You must be willing to ask for help.
- You must be willing to become vulnerable and try something new.

Questions for Reflection

1. When was the last time you were truly seen? What was the situation? What did it feel like? During and after the encounter, how did it make you think about yourself?

2. How would you describe the level of your loneliness after the encounter compared to before the encounter?

3. Do you have someone in your life who makes you feel safe or has the potential to do so?

4. When was the last time you felt emotionally, psychologically, and spiritually safe?

5. Are there adjustments you need to make for this to happen? What past hurts need to be healed for this to happen?

6. In what way are you best soothed?

7. When was the last time you were soothed? What did that experience look like?

Part III

PRACTICAL
SOLUTIONS

7

MODEL FOR ACTION

The Greatest Commandment

The Christian mind is the prerequisite of Christian thinking, and Christian thinking is the prerequisite for Christian action.
HARRY BLAMIRES

I LOVE TO FISH. For most of my life, I've fished with bait or a louver from the shore of a lake. My grandfather loved to fish, and many of my memories with him are of us fishing on a lake or a river. There's something so peaceful and calming about being out in nature, casting a line into the water, and patiently waiting for a fish to bite.

When my grandfather passed away ten years ago, I inherited one of his bamboo fly-fishing rods. For years, it sat in my garage in an aluminum cylindrical tube. When we moved into our new home, I found the rod as I was unpacking, and my interest in fly fishing began. I started researching all aspects of fly fishing. I learned about the rod and the reel, and I studied what type of line is needed for the different types of rivers and fish. I watched count-less videos on how to tie a proper fly and which fly would work best for the specific river I was fishing. I watched videos from some of the best fishermen and women in the world on how to properly cast a line, and in the summer of 2019, I went to a fly-fishing club with a dear friend and had a two-day lesson from an experienced river guide. Fly fishing became my new hobby.

What if I told you that that's as far as I went with my fly-fishing hobby? That I invested all this time, effort, and money into it, but I never put my rod in the river on my own? This would be pretty ridiculous, right? But far too often, this is what we do as a human race. We collect "good" information and then never do anything with it.

We've covered a lot of information in the first two parts of this book, and I hope you've been challenged and inspired. If we ended the book at the completion of Part II, it'd be a useless book. We must put into practical action the things we've discussed, or the learned information doesn't matter. Consider the words of James: "*Act* on what you hear! Those who hear and don't act are like those who glance in the mirror, walk away, and two minutes later have no idea who they are, what they look like" (James 1:22-23).

Part III will be this practical and experiential engagement with the previous sections. I encourage you to enter this section with an open mind. Growth and change can be difficult at first, but they're almost always restorative.

You Shouldn't Always Rely on Professionals

Far too often, I've clients who come into my office wanting me to fix their problem. Typically, I'll sit back in my chair and ask this question: "What would it accomplish if I fixed your problem?"

Most often, their response is "Well, I'd be cured" or "I'd feel better." I follow their reasoning for a moment, and it almost always comes down to the conclusion that they're uncertain of the work that they'll need to personally do to engage in and change the problem they're facing. As a counselor, I could easily give them advice, but the outcome would be the same. They'd "get better" for a moment and then be right back in my office when the next problem happened. It's my job as a counselor to walk alongside the client, partner with them, equip, empower, and encourage them toward necessary changes. Here's the catch: They need to make these changes themselves, or change won't last.

Do you see where I'm going here? I could tell you what to do to change the loneliness inside you and those around you, or I could partner, equip, empower, and encourage you in actively taking up the mantle of change. When each of us makes this commitment to change, we're making a statement that we (individually and collectively) are willing to do the personal and collaborative work necessary to eradicate this loneliness epidemic. Will you, right now, commit to purposively, intentionally, and mindfully work through the remainder of this book with an open mind and a teachable spirit? I truly believe we can reverse the trajectory of loneliness in our culture, but it'll take all of us to change this insidious tide. Are you willing to do what it takes?

I've alluded to the fact that change must occur in us, in you and me, first. I'll unpack this in greater detail in chapter 8. What I'll say now is this: Make sure you're prepared for this beautiful and difficult journey. You'll take a deep look into the depths of your soul, you'll be asked to reflect on things you probably haven't reflected on before, and you'll be asked to refine areas of your life that likely haven't been uncovered or engaged in years, if ever.

As your guide in this process, I want you to consider several things prior to embarking on this epic journey with me.

Are you teachable? Being teachable means recognizing you have more to learn. Someone who is teachable adopts an open posture of curiosity, learning, and humility. Look at the story of Mary and Martha in Luke's Gospel (Luke 10:38-42). Mary's posture was one of openness and curiosity. She sat at Jesus' feet and intently listened to his words. She was ready to learn. Martha, on the other hand, was busy working and doing—which is not wrong, but she missed out on the learning. Being teachable means slowing down, learning to be still, reflecting, listening, and adjusting things in your personal life prior to doing. After a while, with some practice, being and doing can become interchangeable, allowing teachability to become a state of mind.

Are you willing to be vulnerable? Opening the recesses of your soul to anyone is a scary proposition. For the time being, I'm only asking you to do this with God. To truly be vulnerable, you have to be honest and transparent with yourself and with God. I don't know if you do this, but when I'm in devotion or prayer time with the Lord, I have the tendency to justify my thoughts and behaviors. It's not as if God doesn't already know the deep recesses of my soul. Psalm 139:7-12 reminds us of this:

> Is there anyplace I can go to avoid your Spirit?
>   to be out of your sight?
> If I climb to the sky, you're there!
>   If I go underground, you're there!

If I flew on morning's wings
    to the far western horizon,
You'd find me in a minute—
    you're already there waiting!
Then I said to myself, "Oh, he even sees me in the dark!
    At night I'm immersed in the light!"
It's a fact: darkness isn't dark to you;
      night and day, darkness and light, they're all the same
        to you.

Hiding the truths of our struggles only makes us more miserable and alone. True vulnerability is bringing who we are—our current struggles, pains, emotions, and fears—into congruence with what God already knows. When that alignment happens, true change can begin.

The combination of teachability and vulnerability will rightly position you for growth and change. Embrace the uncertainty and ambiguity with me, and engage the beauty of the struggle. For, as with Jacob in the Old Testament (Genesis 32:22-32), it's in the wrestling that true blessing will occur.

A Biblical Model for Reflective Change

I'll admit that I'm guilty of trying to figure things out myself. The "I do it!" mentality runs deep within me. The older I get, the quicker I'm able to remember that there's likely a better way to do things, and I don't have to make a mistake to learn. The Bible is a deep well of wisdom and should be the first place we turn when we have a problem or question. While researching for this book, I spent a lot of time poring over the Scriptures, reading commentaries, and exploring the beauty and depth of the original language.

I wasn't looking for a passage of Scripture to fit my point; rather, I was looking for a model that could help me navigate the process of realigning our lost relationships.

In the process of poring over the Scriptures, I was reintroduced to the greatest commandment, found in Matthew 22. I was excited to find a framework we can use in eradicating this loneliness epidemic. Matthew 22:36-40 states:

> When the Pharisees heard how he had bested the
> Sadducees, they gathered their forces for an assault.
> One of their religion scholars spoke for them, posing
> a question they hoped would show him up: "Teacher,
> which command in God's Law is the most important?"
> Jesus said, "'Love the Lord your God with all your
> passion and prayer and intelligence.' This is the most
> important, the first on any list. But there is a second to
> set alongside it: 'Love others as well as you love yourself.'
> These two commands are pegs; everything in God's Law
> and the Prophets hangs from them."

I grew up memorizing this passage, but I don't think I truly understood the depth of its meaning until I was able to dive into the original text and context.

The religious leaders were trying to catch Jesus in a theological trap. As scholars of the Old Testament, they were looking at the Levitical law and the Ten Commandments. The theological trap was that the Jewish scholars had ordered the commandments into greater and smaller orders of importance but hadn't yet determined which one was of the greatest priority. Jesus goes around this argument by quoting from the Shema: "Attention, Israel! GOD, our

God! GOD the one and only! Love GOD, your God, with your whole heart: love him with all that's in you, love him with all you've got" (Deuteronomy 6:4-5). He then adds the command to love others as well as we love ourselves. Let's spend just a moment breaking down verses 37-40 of Matthew 22.

> [Jesus said,] "'Love the Lord your God with all your passion [heart] and prayer [soul] and intelligence [mind].' This is the most important, the first on any list."

The first part of this passage focuses on our need and duty to love God. The word for love here is the verb *agapaō*, defined as the action of love and the ability to take pleasure in. It's not a sedentary love but a love of action. The action comes in loving God with all our passion. The word all (*holos*) signifies the entirety of, and heart (*kardia*) signifies the mind, character, and inner self. *Kardia* is mentioned over eight hundred times in Scripture and never refers to the physical organ.[1]

Next we're to love God with our prayer (soul). The Greek word for soul is *psuchē* or *syche*, which is our vital breath of life. Finally, we're to love God with all our intelligence (mind). Mind (*dianoia*) refers to disposition, intellect, and thought. So, in verses 37 and 38, we're commanded to love God with the entirety of our inner selves—our vital breath of life, our disposition, and our intellect.

This act of complete love is the first and greatest commandment, but Jesus doesn't stop there. He says in verse 39, "But there is a second to set alongside it: 'Love others as well as you love yourself.'"

I don't know about you, but in my linear, list-making, Western mind, I ordered these. First, love God; check. Second, love others; check. Finally, if I get around to it, love self. But guess what?

I very rarely get around to loving myself. Going deeper, I found something very interesting, something you would not typically notice while reading an English translation of this verse. The phrase "a second to set alongside it" (or, in other translations, "the second is like it") has a different meaning than just an ordered list.

The phrase "alongside" or "like it" is the Greek word *homoios*, which means resembling, similar to, or equal to. Therefore, *loving others and self is just as important as loving God*. The word for love in this passage is the same Greek word, *agapaō*—whoa!

Jesus goes on to say that everything depends on this. Instead of an ordered list that needs to be checked off, I now view this as a symbiotic, reciprocal relationship, whereby we must honestly reflect on how well we love God, others, and self. If any one of these gets out of alignment, it'll affect the others. Can we truly love God with all our heart, soul, and mind if we don't love others and self well? Can we love others and self well if we don't love God well?

The remainder of Part III explores the components of this symbiotic, cyclical, and reciprocal framework. In chapter 8, we'll examine the idea of loving self and God and how it can affect relational loneliness and isolation. In chapter 9, we'll look at the importance of loving others. Chapter 10 investigates the church's responsibility, and finally, chapter 11 ties it all together in one messy embrace.

Questions for Reflection

1. How would you rate your vulnerability on a scale of 1 to 10, where 1 means "I never put myself in a position to feel vulnerable" and 10 means "I'm comfortable with being vulnerable when I feel it's appropriate to do so"? How would you rate your teachability?

2. Reflect on Matthew 22:37-40. What are your thoughts and feelings about this passage?

3. Does this new revelation change how you see God, others, and yourself? If so, how? If not, why?

8

INDIVIDUAL RESPONSIBILITY

Looking Inward

The hill, though high, I covet to ascend,
The difficulty will not me offend;
For I perceive the way to life lies here.
Come, pluck up heart, let's neither faint nor fear;
Better, though difficult, the right way to go,
Than wrong, though easy, where the end is woe.
JOHN BUNYAN, *The Pilgrim's Progress*

I TRAVELED A LOT in my late teens and early twenties. Most of my traveling was done on mission trips to help those less fortunate. I went on one trip to an American Indian reservation in southern Montana. I was going into my senior year of high school at the time. The trip to the reservation was straightforward. We were to travel via fifteen-passenger van, north on Interstate 25 through Wyoming to southern Montana. The drive north was simple and uneventful. So it'd be safe to assume that the drive home would be just as uneventful, right?

Well, my youth pastor, Brian, had just purchased a new GPS system. (This was in the mid-1990s, so this was a big deal.) He thought he'd use it to try to find a more direct route home. It didn't go as planned, as the GPS rerouted us through South Dakota.

I remember waking up from a nap and looking out the window, wondering where we were. As my eyes adjusted, I saw pine trees and hills whizzing by. (For those of you who don't know, central and eastern Wyoming don't have a whole lot to look at—just a lot of open prairie.) We'd made a wrong turn where Interstate 25 and Interstate 90 intersect and went southeast instead of south.

Fortunately, our detour allowed me to see Mount Rushmore, but what was supposed to be a seven-and-a-half-hour trip turned into an over-fifteen-hour trip. If my youth pastor had paid attention to his surroundings and zoomed out on his GPS, he would've seen the bigger picture and made adjustments.

The more information we have, the more informed we are. Hopefully, the more informed we are, the better decisions we make. I truly believe this is the case when it comes to our relationship with God. It's way too easy to zoom in and focus on the extremes of our pain, disappointment, and loneliness. If we don't zoom out, we struggle to engage anything in our full view. If you put your hand right in front of your face and then tried to walk through the grocery store, it'd be impossible not to trip over something. To effectively navigate, we have to see clearly, and to see clearly, we need to see the bigger picture. This also needs to happen in our relationship with God. It can be so easy to blame God for our mental, emotional, physical, and spiritual struggles. I've fallen into this trap. It's the original lie, repurposed from the Fall.

We've already explored the origins of sin and relational separation in Genesis 3. Zooming out, did you know that the story of rescue and redemption entered the picture at the same time? I did a word study in the original Greek and Hebrew to see if I could find the word for relationship, thinking it'd be the antithesis of loneliness and separation. What I found brought me to tears.

Instead of a word for relationship, I found the Hebrew word *ga'al*, which is the word for redemption and, by implication, relationship. *Ga'al* means to redeem from bondage, to rescue, or to purchase something of value. Focusing in on the Greek, the verb *lutroo* means to release by paying a ransom, and *lytroō* means to restore something or someone to the possession of the rightful owner, rescuing from an alien possessor. The closest words to relationship that I found were *yhiothesia*, the word for adoption; *huios*, the word for descendent; and *suggeneia*, the word for kinship, which is derived from the word *ginomai*, which means to become and signifies a change of condition or state, implying motion and growth.

Let's connect the dots. The moment relational separation and loneliness entered the picture is the exact moment redemption entered the picture. Zooming out, we can see that Satan's lie is a distraction, a hand in the face, from the bigger picture of rescue and redemption. So why do we continue to believe the lie of loneliness and separation instead of the truth of redemption? For many of us, it's because no one has shown us the way to confront these lies.

Stepping Up to the Challenge

I've been working with people all my adult life. I've been in the messiness of the trenches, walking with people through their traumas, their deepest hurts and wounding. I've heard some rough stories, things I wouldn't dream of putting on paper. For the most part, I can compartmentalize these horrific stories and sit with people in their pain and suffering, taking on the role of guide, sage, and friend. But what gets me every time is when a client wonders what they've accomplished in their life. Most often, the counseling room becomes filled with a deep sense of loneliness and sadness.

Many of these clients also feel a depth of hopelessness that latches on and whispers, *This is the way it will always be*. Sadly, many individuals choose to believe this lie.

I'm here to tell you that isn't the case. It *can* change, and there *is* hope. It'll be messy, and it'll be hard. But it can be so good!

In my experience, there are two types of people: those who run into a challenge and those who run from or are frozen by a challenge. Individuals who run into a challenge have a unique set of characteristics that adequately prepare them for what lies ahead (I touched on a couple of these earlier in the book):

- *They recognize the importance of growth.* Far too often, I get individuals in my office who are seeking counseling because their lives are falling apart, but instead of looking for ways to grow, they want to sit in their struggle and blame others. For growth to happen, you must first recognize its value.

- *They have a growth mindset.* Growth isn't only important; it's possible. Having a growth mindset means you recognize you don't have it all figured out but that you have the skill needed to move forward. This is different from having a fixed mindset, where you don't believe change or growth can happen.

- *There is an innate, reflective honesty about them.* This speaks for itself.

- *They don't back down when things get hard.* Fortitude and perseverance are key characteristics. They've developed grit and resiliency. They've found the ability to push through when things get tough.

- *They're humble.* The opposite of proud!

- *They're teachable.* Can you take correction? Are you able to admit when you're wrong?

- *They have a basic understanding of change and aren't afraid to make necessary adjustments.* This might sound like a big task, but I'll break down the stages of change here so that you have a deeper, more comprehensive understanding.

You may have a preconceived notion that those who run straight toward challenges they face are invincible and perfect. Realistically, this isn't the case; however, these individuals do have a deep sense of flexibility and a readiness for things to be different. They can take a step back, reflect, and adjust. They can assess the situation and make necessary changes. And they can admit when they're wrong.

Conversely, individuals who run away or are frozen by challenges also have a distinct set of characteristics:

- They have a fixed mindset.
- They easily latch on to the victim mentality.
- They don't think they need to change or that anything is wrong.
- They have an excuse for everything.
- They aren't teachable.
- Resiliency and grit are foreign concepts.
- They give up or place blame when things don't go their way.
- Fear is their master.
- They're afraid of change and unwilling to make necessary adjustments.

Which of these do you identify with most? Be honest; no one is watching or judging you. Read over the descriptions one more time. This honest reflection, right here, right now, will determine how you engage in your own loneliness—and eventually, how you'll engage in the loneliness of those around you.

A Barrier to Change

Before I expound on characteristics of individuals who confront their challenges, I thought it'd be prudent to discuss a big barrier to change: our own stories.

Several years ago, Sarah and I were able to take our girls to Disney World. It was a quick trip for my doctorate graduation in Orlando, and we took the opportunity of being so close to Disney World. I was so excited to take the girls to "the most magical place on earth." When I was growing up in central California, my family ventured to Disneyland a time or two, but I'd never been to Disney World. I loved the thrill of roller coasters and the excitement of the park itself.

What I couldn't stand was the teacup ride. The constant spinning tied my insides in knots. I did my best to steer my girls away from the teacups at Disney World, but sure enough, when they saw them, they were determined to go on them. I couldn't say no, so I reluctantly got on with them. At first, the ride wasn't so bad, but as we picked up speed by turning the little wheel in the middle, we started spinning out of control.

The out-of-control spinning felt very familiar, like the negative cycle of my story swirling around in my head. I was burdened by my story. For years after my suicide attempt, I was ashamed to discuss what had happened. The suicidal thoughts were gone, but how I thought of myself didn't change much. For many years, I was stuck in the cycle of self-doubt, condemnation, fear, and shame. I felt that, as a human being, I was flawed in many ways.

Due to my maladaptive thought patterns, I unknowingly listened to the "cycle of stories" in my head, and as I did, the world around me seemed to confirm how I viewed myself. This Story Cycle kept me stuck in a lie. I didn't have a right understanding of self, nor did I have a right understanding of God. The result was loneliness.

The first step in confronting the loneliness epidemic is an honest reflection of self in relationship to God. To make this experience beneficial, I encourage you to use a journal in conjunction with this chapter as a place to engage your thoughts, emotions, and ideas. Don't fall into the trap of thinking that what you write has to be perfect. Instead, allow yourself to be messy, honest, and vulnerable.

Before I move on to explore the characteristics of individuals who embrace challenges, it'd be beneficial for you to explore your own Story Cycle. A Story Cycle is self-perpetuating: We settle on a recurring narrative (a foundational thought or defining story) for ourselves and ruminate on it. This narrative comes to shape our basic beliefs about ourselves. The more we seep ourselves in these basic beliefs, the more our identity becomes anchored in them—*we become what we believe about ourselves.* And having become this identity, we project the narrative out into the world as something fixed and final: We expect the dynamic of the first narrative to be present in every other narrative. Because of confirmation bias, we're affirmed in these expectations, and our narrative is reasserted and reinforced. And the cycle repeats itself until something interrupts it (see Figure 5). Pull out your journal and follow along with my example, then I'll have you reflect on your own Story Cycle.

1. *Hear It or Tell It to Ourselves*: My reoccurring narrative was that I was a loser, that I was worthless.

2. *Believe It*: As I ruminated on these thoughts, I began to believe them: *I believe I'm a loser and that I'm worthless.*

3. *Behave like It / Become It*: The more I believed these lies, the more I became them: *I'm a worthless loser.*

4. *Expect It*: The more I became the stories, the more I "saw" them in the world around me: *Everyone else thinks I'm a worthless loser too.*

5. The cycle comes full circle and reaffirms the thoughts and stories: *See—I'm right. I'm a worthless loser.*

Story Cycle

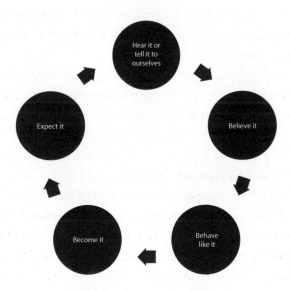

Take some time to explore your own Story Cycle. I don't want you to give the "right" answer; I want you to give the honest answer. *The only way change will take place is if you're honest with yourself.*

This may initially be a difficult process, but it'll be a freeing one. Take some time to explore your own Story Cycle by interacting with the following questions in a journal.

- What words, thoughts, or stories are common themes in your life? (It could be something that you heard growing up, or it could be something you concluded about yourself.) Write them down.
- What beliefs arose from those thoughts?
- How has that shaped your identity?
- How has that shaped your relationships?

Fill in the blanks to reveal your own Story Cycle. What emotions and thoughts come up as you reflect on your Story Cycle? Write those down.

For many of you, this is the first time you've taken the time to reflect on your Story Cycle. It can be an overwhelming experience. My encouragement to you is that it can change—and you have the power to change it!

Confronting the Loneliness Within

Remaining in our maladaptive Story Cycles may seem like the only option. Believing that there's no other option than thinking of ourselves negatively is just repurposing of the same lie we found at the beginning of the human story. Conventional, worldly wisdom would have us believe that we have all the answers, that if we look inside ourselves, then we can rightly order everything around us. But God's wisdom is countercultural. God's wisdom tells us to look outside ourselves for the answers, to look to and focus our attention on him.

The first step to healing is obtaining a proper love of self—but to have a proper love of self, we must first have a proper love of God. "Love the Lord your God with all your passion and prayer and intelligence. . . . the first on any list." To love God with our passion, prayer, and intelligence, we must view loving God as a choice and a discipline rather than a feeling. If we only loved God when we felt like it, we never would. The idea is that we strive hard to love God with our whole being, our vital breath of life, and our every thought. This is a good proposition, but it isn't an easy one. It takes intentionality and discipline. There is no formula.

I've belonged to many churches in my life that have—intentionally or unintentionally—used shame to get me to have a relationship with God. They created a formula for me: memorize Scripture + read the Bible for a least two hours per day + get up at 4:00 a.m. and pray for four hours = a relationship with God. Yes, these are good disciplines, but I felt like if I didn't do them just right, I was a bad or deficient Christian, which effactually put me back in my negative Story Cycle.

Instead, I began to read the greatest commandment as an invitation and a command. Pair this with it also being a choice and a discipline, and you start to see that God invites us to love him with our whole being. His wisdom shows us that if we choose to love him in this way, the ability to love ourselves becomes a little bit easier, allowing the deep hurt within to begin healing. The more we intentionally enter his presence, the more the chasm of loneliness dissipates.

Steps Toward Healing

Allowing ourselves to heal from loneliness can seem like a daunting task. Many of us haven't started this process because we didn't know where to begin. Everyone's journey will be different, but it's important to consider three steps in this process.

Before I introduce the three steps, I want you to know that you'll likely hit roadblocks on the journey toward healing. When you do, stop where you are, step back from the process, take a deep breath, and pray against any distraction or lie that may try to creep in. A simple but effective prayer could be something like this:

> In the strong name of Jesus and by the power of his
> blood shed on the Cross for me, I pray against the spirit
> of _____ (*fear, confusion, anxiety, etc.*).

Calling out what's happening or what you're feeling in that moment will allow you to realign your mindset. Don't let the possible frustration of the process deter you from pushing through. When therapy gets hard, I tell my clients that the pain of working through the struggle is much more refining than the pain of staying in the struggle.

Step One: Acknowledge the Loneliness You're Facing

It's amazing to me that as a human race, we can attempt to deny or ignore the reality of truth that's right in front of us. I can't tell you how many times I've heard the statement: "If I don't acknowledge it, it doesn't exist." Why do we do that? It's similar to being diagnosed with stage-four pancreatic cancer and refusing to acknowledge or do anything about it. This seems like a ridiculous thing to do, but we do it all the time.

One way to confront and acknowledge our loneliness within is to reflect on our mental, emotional, physical, and spiritual health. Remember from Part I that the quality of these four areas can be linked to the amount of loneliness and isolation in our lives. Take some time and utilize your journal to answer these questions, first focusing on mental health:

1. How would you describe your mental health?
2. In what way is your mental health flourishing?
3. In what way is your mental health struggling?
4. What are some actionable steps you could take to improve your mental health?

Now reflect on your emotional health.

1. How would you rate your emotional health?
2. What is your emotional intelligence? (Some surveys that can help you assess your emotional intelligence can be found at www.ihhp.com/free-eq-quiz/ and https://www.psychologytoday.com/us/tests/personality /emotional-intelligence-test.)
3. What were your emotional models?
4. How were emotions experienced in your house growing up?
5. How do you deal with emotions in your life today?
6. What are the main emotions you feel on a regular basis?
7. What would you like to change about your emotional health and intelligence?

Move on now to your physical health.

1. How is your physical health? On a scale of 1 (not healthy) to 10 (healthy), how would you rate yourself?

2. What physical ailments are you currently struggling with?

3. What can you do to change your physical health? Do you need to change how you eat or how much you move? Do you need to readjust your sleep?

4. If you had a magic wand and could change your physical health, what would you want to be different?

And finally, give attention to your spiritual health.

1. How would you describe your spirituality?

2. What defines your spirituality?

3. How would you rate your relationship with God on a scale of 1 (not close) to 10 (close)? Why?

4. What would you want to change?

Now take a step back and reflect on your answers. What themes arise from your notes? Are you seeing patterns of loneliness or isolation? It's okay if you are, but you need to acknowledge the reality of it if you want anything to change.

Step Two: Take Ownership of Changing Your Path

Now that you've acknowledged your loneliness, you have a crossroads decision to make. You can either ignore what you've discovered or take ownership of it. One path leads to denial and further isolation and loneliness. The other path leads to lasting change.

Ownership means it is no one else's burden to carry, nor is it someone else's problem. Yes, you can search for and find support systems on this journey, but this change is between you and God.

The lie is that we're all by ourselves to figure this out. In Matthew 11:28-30, Jesus says,

> Are you tired? Worn out? Burned out on religion? Come to me. Get away with me and you'll recover your life. I'll show you how to take a real rest. Walk with me and work with me—watch how I do it. Learn unforced rhythms of grace. I won't lay anything heavy or ill-fitting on you. Keep company with me and you'll learn to live freely and lightly.

This is a promise and a beautiful reminder of the relationship Jesus wants to have with us. Once we take ownership of the problem, we have the promise, support, and guidance of God with us.

Step Three: Actively Use the Tools Given to Enact Necessary Change

A mechanic wouldn't use a rolling pin to change the oil in your car, nor would a chef use a wrench to whip egg whites. You need the proper tools to get the job done. Different jobs require different tools. When working toward healing in your loneliness journey, you'll need to practice honesty, vulnerability, reflection, and awareness.

The characteristics I mentioned at the beginning of this chapter can also be viewed as tools. Each tool is a resource to aid in healing loneliness. If you're lacking in one of these tools, find ways to grow and strengthen yourself. I've provided a resource and reading list for you at the end of this book; use it if you'd like to grow in any of these areas. As you read through these tools, I'll challenge you to rate yourself on a scale of 1 (needs work) to 10 (strong).

Remember that we all have areas of growth, so be honest in your self-assessment.

Tool #1: A Growth Mindset: A growth mindset is the opposite of a fixed mindset. If you have a fixed mindset, you believe that the skills, abilities, emotions, et cetera that you're born with is as good as it's going to get and that there's no room for growth or change. If you have a growth mindset, you're able to recognize your strengths and weaknesses, and you realize that with hard work and persistence, you can develop your skills and abilities.

Tool #2: Reflective Honesty: Reflective honesty is the ability to reflect on past decisions and events and accurately evaluate them.

Tool #3: Grit: Grit is simply mental and emotional toughness. If you have grit, when something gets hard, you don't give up.

Tool #4: Resiliency: Resiliency is the ability to get back up after you have fallen, faltered, struggled, or made a mistake.

Tool #5: Humility: Humility is the ability and willingness to admit when you're wrong.

Tool #6: Teachability: Teachability is the willingness to learn from your mistakes and from others who are further along on the journey.

Tool #7: Ability to Embrace Change: Embracing change is not rocket science, yet it has to be deliberate. In our humanness, we'll want to run from change, so change must be a methodical, cognitive choice.

The Antithesis of Loneliness

Antithetical to loneliness are three concepts that seem very simple on paper but can be very difficult to practice. There is no perfect or easy way to engage these three concepts. They'll constantly change, and it'll be hard, yet it'll be good, and you'll find freedom. You must be prepared for this journey (yes, it'll be a journey and a process, not a singular moment in time). You'll get dirty, stumble, and want to give up. But everything good is worth fighting for. In his classic book *The Pilgrim's Progress*, John Bunyan depicted this concept quite well: "The hill, though high, I covet to ascend, / The difficulty will not me offend; / For I perceive the way to life lies here. / Come, pluck up heart, let's neither faint nor fear; / Better, though difficult, the right way to go, / Than wrong, though easy, where the end is woe."[1]

The sad fact is that many of us don't engage the difficult, necessary, and good journey until our world falls apart. Many years ago, a client sought me out for counseling because her world was falling apart. She couldn't hold together the smoke and mirrors, the facade of her life, any longer. The harder she tried to control her world, the worse her situation became. Erin was a very successful businesswoman in her mid-to-late forties. She was a self-made millionaire and the CEO of a major company. Erin grew up in a poor family from Kentucky. "My dad never finished high school, and my mom never made it past the sixth grade," Erin stated in one of our sessions. "My dad was a journeyman carpenter and always had a difficult time finding and keeping a job. I remember times when we had to skip eating for a day or two just to make sure our bills were paid."

Erin went on to describe the verbal and emotional abuse she received at the hand of her father. "He very rarely hit me, maybe once or twice, but he was ruthless with his mouth. He would scream, call us names, and threaten us on a daily basis. As I got older, he began to drink more, and the abuse became worse." Erin told me that, at eighteen, she left the house, promising herself that she'd never be as lonely and miserable as her father: "I told myself that I'd never follow in my father's footsteps. I'd finish college, get a good job, and make something of myself. I didn't want to ever be like him!" She paused for a minute, then looked up at me with tears welling up in her eyes. "But here I am thirty years later—successful, wealthy, and just as lonely as him. Where did I go wrong?"

Sadly, Erin's story is not unique. I hear and see this all the time. Erin had done a good job of filling the void of loneliness with the busyness of success, and for a little while, she thought she was one step ahead of it. But if we don't deal with the root of our problems, it'll eventually creep back up and consume us. Therefore, we must push through the pretense and engage the antithesis of loneliness: identity, purpose, and hope. Only when we engage these three things will the chasm of loneliness begin to be filled.

The first step in this journey is exploring our *identity*. I don't know about you, but the existential question of *Who am I?* strikes fear in my heart. I can't just spout off things that I do, my profession, or a list of my accomplishments. *Who am I?* goes much deeper than that. I was eighteen when I started college, and I thought I knew who I was. I quickly realized how wrong I was. I was determined to have my college experience be different from my middle school and high school experiences. So I made the cognitive decision to say yes to as many things as possible. The only problem with this mindset is that I didn't know who I was or what I liked. As a result, I fell deeper into despair, which is linked to loneliness. It wasn't until I entered my master's program that I began to unpack and explore this existential question.

Why is this question so important? I believe it's one of the main catalysts in eliminating loneliness from your life. If you can answer it with confidence and resolve, you won't be swayed by the changing tides of culture, politics, religion, pop culture, and the like. Dutch theologian Henri Nouwen indicated that there are three typical answers to this question:

- I am what I do;
- I am what others say about me; or
- I am what I have.[2]

Basically, Nouwen was saying that our modern culture answers this question by externalizing it rather than internalizing it. To internalize this question, we must open all aspects of who we are to the light of who God is. We need to be 100 percent transparent in how we approach this question.

Go back and look at your Story Cycle. You're going to use it to rework your story. Identity is the foundation from which everything else can be built. I'm challenging you to consider the question "Whose are you?" rather than "Who am I?" Pull out your journal and explore these key Scripture passages:

- *2 Corinthians 5:17*: a new creation
- *2 Peter 1:4*: partakers of the divine nature
- *Ephesians 2:1-5*: dead in our trespasses and sin but alive in Christ

- *Romans 6:4-6*: walking in newness of life, no longer a slave to sin
- *Romans 8:1*: free from condemnation
- *Romans 8:29*: conformed to his image
- *Ephesians 1:3*: blessed with every spiritual blessing

These are just a couple of examples of Scriptures that speak identity over us. There are many more through the New Testament, and they all do one thing: They remind us, you and me, that loneliness and separation from God are a lie. He has purposefully redeemed us and adopted us as his sons and daughters. Our identity is not outside of ourselves but, rather, inside each of our souls as a representation of what Christ did for us on the Cross.

The first step is choosing the free gift of salvation that Christ offers and allowing him to speak the truth of who we are over us. After that, it's our job to willfully and intentionally remind ourselves of this truth and not get sidetracked by the lies around us.

The next step in eradicating loneliness is finding our *purpose*. Purpose naturally flows out of our identity and allows us to engage the world around us with meaning. When I started to realize and believe that I was a cherished, redeemed, and adopted son of the Most High God, I found confidence and strength in who I am. I cared less about what others thought of me (though this can still be a challenge), and I found my foundational security in Christ. From this strength and confidence came my passion and my purpose.

I love working with and caring for people. I'm intrigued by our mental, emotional, physical, and spiritual health and passionate about bringing people back into proper alignment. This book, for example, is a product of my passion and purpose.

I must be very clear: Purpose must always flow from identity.

If it doesn't, it has the potential to create pride or codependency (people pleasing). Identity (in Christ) and purpose must be consistently reflected on and calibrated to make sure they are properly balanced.

Finally, *hope*. Without hope, we have nothing. As believers, we find hope in Jesus Christ and his blood, shed on the Cross for our sins. Hope is central to the gospel, and it's central to eliminating loneliness. Hope is the ability to look up and see beyond current circumstances, pain, turmoil, and disappointments to what lies ahead. The original lie will shout, *It will always be this way!* But hope will whisper quietly, *It's okay. Keep going; it will get better.* Hope is exemplified in the twenty-third Psalm:

GOD, my shepherd!
    I don't need a thing.
You have bedded me down in lush meadows,
    you find me quiet pools to drink from.
True to your word,
    you let me catch my breath
    and send me in the right direction.

Even when the way goes through
    Death Valley,
I'm not afraid
    when you walk at my side.
Your trusty shepherd's crook
    makes me feel secure.

You serve me a six-course dinner
    right in front of my enemies.

You revive my drooping head;
    my cup brims with blessing.

Your beauty and love chase after me
    every day of my life.
I'm back home in the house of GOD
    for the rest of my life.

Our present, future, and eternal hope is wrapped up in this passage. It speaks to our identity, our purpose, and our hope.

The Difference between Loneliness and Solitude

Before I conclude this chapter, I want to make a clear distinction: Loneliness is not solitude, and solitude is not loneliness. As we have discussed, loneliness is a state of being unseen or unnoticed relationally, mentally, emotionally, physically, and/or spiritually. It can be driven by lack of purpose or meaning, relationship, and/or identity and is marked by a deep sense of hopelessness. Solitude, on the other hand, is a by-product of discovering identity, purpose, and hope. Henri Nouwen stated:

> We enter into solitude first of all to meet our Lord and to be with him and him alone. . . . Only in the context of grace can we face our sin; only in the place of healing do we dare to show our wounds; only with a single-minded attention to Christ can we give up our clinging fears and face our own true nature. . . .
>
> . . . Solitude is . . . the place where Christ remodels us in his own image and frees us from the victimizing compulsions of the world.[3]

Loneliness happens in the chaos and noise of this world. Solitude can only be found in purposeful silence. If we aren't careful, loneliness will creep up on us; therefore, it's important to engage in the discipline of solitude so that we can be reminded of our identity, purpose, and hope.

Questions for Reflection

1. How does it feel to realize that *redemption* is the word for relationship?

2. What are your thoughts about redemption being part of the story all along?

3. How has your Story Cycle affected how you see yourself and the world around you?

4. What can you do to reclaim and realign your Story Cycle?

5. Have you given much thought to Whose you are?

6. Have you considered what your purpose is?

7. Do you have the hope of a saving relationship with Jesus Christ?

If this is the first time you've ever heard the gospel (Good News) of Jesus Christ, I ask you to pray this prayer with me.

Jesus, I need hope. I recognize that I've made a lot of mistakes in my life and that I can't continue doing this on my own. I'm lonely, and I need you. Please forgive me of my pride and sin. Will you come and speak the truth of Whose I am over me?

Recognizing who we are in relation to Whose we are is important. Accepting Jesus Christ into your life is an important step in the process of reclaiming your identity, finding your purpose, and engaging in hope.

PERSONAL RESPONSIBILITY

What Happens When We Are Part of the Solution

Are you upset little friend? Have you been lying awake worrying? Well,
don't worry . . . I'm here. The flood waters will recede, the famine will end,
the sun will shine tomorrow, and I will always be here to take care of you.

CHARLIE BROWN TO SNOOPY, *Peanuts* COMIC STRIP

I HAD TO LEARN THE LESSON the hard way. It wasn't easy,
but I'll remember it for the rest of my life. While I was doing my
clinical internship for my master's degree, working with teenagers
in the juvenile justice system, my world came crashing down. I
had been enjoying the work because I felt like there was still the
ability to help mold and shape them into productive adults. In the
words of my professor, "It isn't too late to change a life when you
work with a child or a teenager." I was 100 percent invested in the
internship and truly felt like I was making an impact. But then
one Monday, as I was getting ready to go into the office, the phone
rang. "Mark?" the voice quivered. "This is Joan. I've got some bad
news." Joan was a probation officer I'd gotten to know over the
course of the past year. "Timothy died last night."

My heart sank. "What?" I exclaimed. "What happened?"

"It looks like he intentionally overdosed," Joan said.

My thoughts started to race. "That can't be right. He was doing so well. He was getting his life together. We'd been working hard on his treatment goals."

My thoughts were abruptly interrupted. "Mark? Are you still there?" Joan asked.

"Yes, I'm still here," I answered quietly. "I just can't believe it! What did I do wrong?"

"Nothing," Joan replied. "You did everything you could."

I'd been working with Timothy for almost a year, and he'd been making such great progress. But more than that, I'd seen such great potential in him. I internalized Timothy's death as my fault. It started to eat away at my confidence as a counselor, and I began questioning my purpose.

My mentor was very observant and saw what was happening to me. "Mark," he said, "you can't own what Timothy chose. It was his decision." He went on to tell me that it was my job to walk alongside my clients—to help guide, challenge, encourage, and empower them. It wasn't my job to work harder than them or lose myself in caring for them. It was a hard lesson, but I needed to learn it, and I'm thankful I learned it early on.

I tell my MA students at Colorado Christian University not to work harder than their clients and that it's not our job to fix our clients or give them advice. The art of counseling is the ability to partner with your client along the road. This is the same advice I'm going to give you. Once you've done the work to confront the loneliness within your own life, the next logical step is wanting to help others do the same. Remember Jesus' words: "But there is a second to set alongside it: 'Love others as well as you love yourself.'" We can't stop at only loving God and loving self; we must complete the cycle and love others well too.

Rhythms versus Balance

I've always hated the word *balance*. I'm not sure why, but when someone tells me I need to balance my life or have "work-life balance," I cringe. I honestly don't think balance is achievable. I used to watch *The Tonight Show Starring Johnny Carson* with my grandparents, and I remember a recurring guest who would spin plates. This guy would start spinning a plate on a tall dowel, then he'd move on to the next dowel and start another plate. After some time, he'd have up to ten plates spinning. That is how I see balance: as a bunch of spinning plates to maintain. We tend to one, get it spinning, then we move to the next one. Our attention becomes divided, and all we're doing is trying to manage the plates. Eventually we're asked to add one more plate, and everything comes crashing down. This was my life for quite some time. I'd do well for a while, and then I'd burn out. All my plates would come crashing down, and I'd have to start over.

I think this is how many of us view the greatest commandment. We think that we have to balance God–Others–Self well. My question is: What if we viewed balance as a cyclical rhythm? In music, rhythm is the ability to sync with the tempo (the rate at which the music moves forward). If the tempo is slower, the rhythm can be more complex and creative. If the tempo is faster, the rhythm must be more simplistic. What if this were how we viewed the greatest commandment—as a series of rhythms to manage? Figure 6 is a basic example.

The slower our life moves forward, the more we can add to our cyclical rhythms. The faster our life moves forward, the less we can add. The constant is that we're maintaining the cyclical rhythms of God–Others–Self. I mention this idea because I've seen

Rhythms

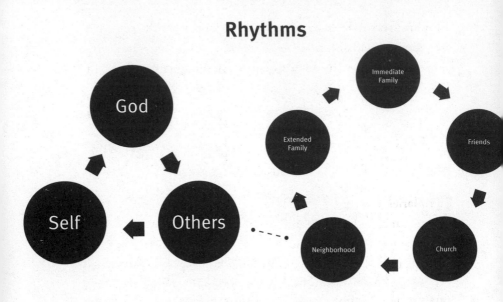

too many well-intentioned people burn out and give up because they can't balance their crazy lives.

Before we get any further into this chapter, I want to introduce you to the stages of change. This concept is important because it'll help you assess how committed to change someone is and how much time and energy you should invest in them. There are six stages of change:

Precontemplation: In this stage, the individual has no intention to alter their current status and no desire for things to be different in the foreseeable future.

Contemplation: The individual desires to change eventually but not yet.

Preparation: The individual is ready to act toward change.

Action: The individual is making the necessary changes and is ready for help and support.

Maintenance: The changes are taking root, and things are
noticeably different.
Termination: In this stage, there's no desire to return to
old ways.[1]

I'd encourage you to reflect on these stages as you enter a relationship or journey with someone out of their loneliness. Boundaries are foundational to the success or failure of this process.

Boundaries

If you don't understand and set boundaries as you walk with
people out of loneliness, you'll fail. I know that this statement is
extreme, but I've seen so many well-intentioned people get burned
out because they don't set appropriate boundaries in this process. I
see boundaries fitting into three categories: fence posts, walls, and
chain-link fences.

Fence Posts: Think about an old, wooden crossbeam fence,
something you'd see at a ranch in the mountains. The fence
hasn't been tended to in years, so the crossbeams have fallen.
All that's left are the posts. Is that still a boundary? Sure, it
marks the property line, but it does nothing to keep someone
from walking from one side to the other. People with fence-
post boundaries tend to be people pleasers who allow others
to walk all over them.

Walls: Sarah and I recently traveled to Wales. While there, we
visited Caerphilly Castle. The castle was majestic in presence
and strength. Surrounding the castle were robust walls made
of stone that were tall, thick, and sturdy. Walls like that were
meant to protect people within the grounds and keep enemies

out. People with wall boundaries are protecting something or trying to keep someone out. These boundaries are the opposite of fence posts; they're very rigid.

Chain-link Fences: I played baseball for many years, and I see this boundary like a backstop. The fence is ten-to-fifteen feet tall and is strong yet flexible. There's one point of entry (through the gate), yet information can still be passed freely through the chain links. Individuals with these types of boundaries are strong, firm, and flexible. Instead of keeping everyone and everything out (like the wall) or letting everyone and everything in (like the fence post), people with chain-link fence boundaries flexibly offer access for healthy relationships and content in their lives.

It's so important to reflect on your boundaries before starting to eradicate loneliness—both your own and others'. Note that it's okay to have different types of boundaries with different types of people. The chain-link fence boundary is the most beneficial and healthy in my opinion, but sometimes it's appropriate to have fence-post or wall boundaries. Consider what type of boundary you lean toward prior to engaging someone in their loneliness journey, and adjust if needed.

The Parable of the Good Samaritan
The parable of the Good Samaritan is a perfect example of what it looks like to love others well while maintaining our individuality. Look at Luke 10:25-37:

> Just then a religion scholar stood up with a question to test Jesus. "Teacher, what do I need to do to get eternal life?"

He answered, "What's written in God's Law? How do you interpret it?"

He said, "That you love the Lord your God with all your passion and prayer and muscle and intelligence— and that you love your neighbor as well as you do yourself."

"Good answer!" said Jesus. "Do it and you'll live."

Looking for a loophole, he asked, "And just how would you define 'neighbor'?"

Jesus answered by telling a story. "There was once a man traveling from Jerusalem to Jericho. On the way he was attacked by robbers. They took his clothes, beat him up, and went off leaving him half-dead. Luckily, a priest was on his way down the same road, but when he saw him he angled across to the other side. Then a Levite religious man showed up; he also avoided the injured man.

"A Samaritan traveling the road came on him. When he saw the man's condition, his heart went out to him. He gave him first aid, disinfecting and bandaging his wounds. Then he lifted him onto his donkey, led him to an inn, and made him comfortable. In the morning he took out two silver coins and gave them to the innkeeper, saying, 'Take good care of him. If it costs any more, put it on my bill—I'll pay you on my way back.'

"What do you think? Which of these three became a neighbor to the man attacked by robbers?"

"The one who treated him kindly," the religion scholar responded.

Jesus said, "Go and do the same."

The first part of this passage appears very familiar: The religious scholars were once again trying hard to trap Jesus in a religious and ethical conundrum. The religious scholar answered correctly the question about salvation and God's law by stating the greatest commandment: "Love the Lord your God with all your passion and prayer and muscle and intelligence—and . . . love your neighbor as well as you do yourself." But he wanted clarification on who the neighbor was.

I find this interesting but not surprising. The religious leaders were trying to find a reason to not care well for people. In their piety, they wanted accolades for doing their duty of loving God well, but they didn't want to complete the rest of the command by loving others well too. I don't know about you, but I can see myself in this situation. I want to look good on the outside, so I quote the right passage and say the right thing, but when it comes down to actually doing the hard things or making a difficult decision to care for someone else, I don't always do the right thing. I want to look good, but I don't want to get dirty. Maybe you can relate.

This Scripture passage is so important for our conversation. I want you to go back and reread the passage with open and honest eyes. Where are you in the story? Are you the man traveling on the road? The priest? The Levite? Or are you the Samaritan? Let's look at each of the main characters in this story:

The Man on the Journey: The man on the journey was most likely Jewish, traveling between Jerusalem and Jericho. He was probably either a businessman, tradesman, or a fisherman. We don't know why he was traveling, but we know he was badly beaten and left for dead. This man represents a lonely individual searching for identity, purpose, and hope.

The Priest: The priest was a respected official from Jerusalem who had just done his priestly duties and was likely headed home. Instead of helping the beaten man, he went to the other side of the road to avoid defilement or getting dirty. This was an intentional, willful avoidance.

The Levite: The Levite was from the Tribe of Levi and was therefore set apart for religious duties. Priests offered sacrifices at the temple, and Levites assisted them. The Levite walked over to the beaten man, looked at him, and didn't want to engage, so he, too, walked around the man and went on his way.

The Priest and the Levite represent those of us who desire to appear "good." We like what this reputation has to offer, and we want to look good doing it. But when it comes down to putting our faith into action, we quickly avoid the messiness of it.

The Samaritan: Samaritans and Jews were so vehemently opposed to each other that they viewed each other as vile creatures. So the Samaritan's actions in the story are a beautiful representation of what it means to care for each other. The Samaritan sees a fellow human hurting and walks up to him. He sees the man's different nationality and religion—*and chooses to ignore the differences and engage the wounded man.* He enters the messiness of this man's distress by cleaning and bandaging him, picking him up onto his donkey, and walking him to the nearby inn. He doesn't just drop him off but pays the innkeeper for his care and then tells him that he'll be back to settle up if additional cost is incurred.

Where do you see yourself in this story? Are you the man beaten and left for dead on the road? If so, it's important that you seek help from a pastor, trusted friend, or counselor. Maybe you're the priest, too busy to be bothered with the messiness of it all. Maybe you're the Levite—concerned and curious, but you don't know where or how to start, so you avoid helping. Maybe you have a heart like the Samaritan and are ready to jump into the trenches and help the hurting individual.

I must say that out of all of these travelers, the Samaritan displayed a confident identity, knew his purpose, and had hope. He didn't care about the stranger's differences in the moment. He saw a fellow human being in need and chose to help.

The Samaritan also had good boundaries. He didn't take the wounded man back to his home but rather to the nearest inn where his care could be dealt with by a third party. The Samaritan is a perfect example of what our response to the hurting and lonely should look like. Be honest with where you are in the story and make the necessary adjustments to (re)align yourself with the mindset and ideals of the Good Samaritan.

Putting It into Practice

Putting these concepts into practice looks good on paper but can be difficult to master, mainly because working with people never is easy or turns out as planned. Furthermore, we humans are innately selfish beings, and it's much easier to avoid getting messy so we can protect ourselves or stay in our comfort zones. Loving others well and adopting the mindset of the Good Samaritan requires us to step outside our bubble and deliberately enter the trenches with people around us. Here are some practical steps to consider as you put this into practice.

First, make sure you're continuing to work on yourself, developing your identity, purpose, and hope. Hurt people hurt people. Another way of saying this is that unhealed wounded people intentionally or unintentionally hurt people. In Matthew 7:1-5, Jesus states:

> Don't pick on people, jump on their failures, criticize their faults—unless, of course, you want the same treatment. That critical spirit has a way of boomeranging. It's easy to see a smudge on your neighbor's face and be oblivious to the ugly sneer on your own. Do you have the nerve to say, "Let me wash your face for you," when your own face is distorted by contempt? It's this whole traveling road-show mentality all over again, playing a holier-than-thou part instead of just living your part. Wipe that ugly sneer off your own face, and you might be fit to offer a washcloth to your neighbor.

It's very clear from this passage that Jesus wants us to take care of our own shortcomings, sin, and woundedness before we engage with anyone else. Therefore, it's essential that you explore your own loneliness first. A big component to counseling is awareness. I often tell my students that it's not about being 100 percent healed from your past, nor is it about being 100 percent perfect in your present; it's about being 100 percent aware of your stuff!

When you're 100 percent aware of your stuff, you won't intentionally or unintentionally blindside someone with a triggered reaction. To be present and effective in entering others' stories and walking with them in their journey toward redemption, you and I must be constantly refining ourselves. Instead of allowing our wounds to hurt others, let's use our experiences and wounds to heal others. Let's be wounded healers instead of wounded hurters.

Next, make sure you're being poured into. We'll talk more about this in chapter 10, but it's important that each of us is operating from an overflowing cup. Yes, we can put a lot of work into our own healing, but it's important to have a mentor, pastor, small group, friend group, meal group, Bible study, counselor, or similar relationship or group of people pouring into us. Remember, we're designed for community, and trying to do this on our own will only burn us out.

Next, make sure you're practicing good self-care. Self-care is essential when working with people. If you and I don't take care of ourselves, we'll burn out. Loving self well means caring for ourselves, resting, and recharging so that we can love others well.

I've been working with people for almost twenty years, mostly as a counselor. I quickly realized that sitting with people in their pain, trauma, woundedness, fear, anxiety, and contempt affects me. Over the years, I've heard some atrocious stories; in fact, not much surprises me anymore. People's stories and experiences will stick to you. Their emotional, mental, and spiritual quantum energy disperses in the room, and it has an impact on counselors. I was determined not to allow that to affect my family, so when I started counseling, I created a self-care regime prior to leaving the office. I pack my gym clothes in a duffle bag and take them with me to the office. Once my last client is done, I wash my hands and face and change out of my work clothes into leisure clothes. This is a symbolic shift that I'm leaving everything at work. It sounds silly, but it really works.

Several years ago, I had the honor of spending some time with John Eldredge. In our conversations and a subsequent training he did for my staff, he talked about the importance of recognizing that each of us has a gravitational field of sin, brokenness, and spiritual warfare. When we work closely with people, their gravitational field has the potential to affect our gravitational field. Therefore, it's important to, as John says, "pray the cross between" you or recite Galatians 6:14:

> For my part, I am going to boast about nothing but the
> Cross of our Master, Jesus Christ. Because of that Cross,
> I have been crucified in relation to the world, set free
> from the stifling atmosphere of pleasing others and fitting
> into the little patterns that they dictate.

It's so important to separate yourself mentally, emotionally, and spiritually from those you choose to journey with.

Similarly, make sure you set good boundaries. You and I are supposed to enter others' processes and support them along their own journey, not fix people or give advice. In *The Lord of the Rings*, the hobbit Frodo is tasked with carrying the most powerful ring from the Shire all the way to Mordor. The journey is perilous, the burden excruciating. There's one part in the story where Frodo can't go any farther. Sam, his faithful friend and companion, exclaims, "Come, Mr. Frodo! I can't carry it for you, but I can carry you and it as well."[2] This is such a beautiful example of what it looks like to walk alongside someone on their journey toward redemption and healing. We must remember that we can never make someone change, but we can be present when they are ready to change.

Many of you reading this book love people deeply and want to see each of them find their best life. That's wonderful. Just

THE PATH OUT OF LONELINESS

remember that you shouldn't be more invested than they are, nor should you work harder than them. The Good Samaritan triaged the man on the road, set up his care, and paid for it. He didn't take the man home, nor did he stay in the same room at the inn and take care of him by himself. He had appropriate boundaries, and so should we.

Finally, make sure you're finding opportunities to step outside your comfort zone. It's human nature to take the path of least resistance and seek comfort. But change can't happen when you and I are comfortable. If we desire to be change agents eradicating loneliness in our world, we must pop our comfort bubbles and try things we've never tried before. This means telling our healing-journey stories and sitting with someone as they work through theirs.

Questions for Reflection

1. Where do you see yourself in the story of the Good Samaritan?

2. What needs to change in your own life for you to become more like the Good Samaritan?

3. How are your rhythms? What needs to be adjusted or changed for you to be healthier?

4. How would you describe your boundaries? What needs to change for you to have healthier boundaries?

5. How would you rate your self-care on a scale of 1 (I never take time for self-care) to 10 (I regularly practice self-care)?

6. What are you doing to step outside your comfort zone?

10

FAITH COMMUNITIES

The Effect of Stepping Outside the Four Walls

I alone cannot change the world, but I can cast a stone
across the waters to create many ripples.

ATTRIBUTED TO MOTHER TERESA

Sometimes we react by a kind of religious reflex and repeat dutifully
the proper words and phrases even though they fail to express our real
feelings and lack the authenticity of personal experience. . . .

. . . This cheerful denial of loneliness proves only that the
speaker has never walked with God without the support
and encouragement afforded him by society.

A. W. TOZER

WHEN I WAS GROWING UP, my emotions overwhelmed me. I was a sensitive kid, and I remember moments when an emotion would wash over me like a wave. I would feel it from the top of my head to the bottom of my toes. It was a scary feeling as a kid, as I couldn't make cognitive sense of what was happening to me. My typical reactions were getting angry or crying.

As I matured, I learned how to manage my reactions, but I never truly learned how to engage my emotions in a healthy way. Going to seminary to become a counselor helped me navigate these emotional waters, but it wasn't until I was introduced to the work of Dr. Elaine Aron that everything started to make sense: I'm a highly sensitive person.

Dr. Aron identified the trait of high sensitivity and coined the phrase "highly sensitive person," which can be defined as "someone who experiences acute physical, mental, or emotional responses to stimuli."[1] Essentially, a highly sensitive person feels things more strongly than others do. They have a heightened sense of awareness, a sixth sense. Mine was emotional. Reading Dr. Aron's work was so freeing; its words put a name to what I'd been experiencing my whole life. It freed me from thinking that something was wrong or broken inside me. In fact, quite the contrary. This emotional sixth sense has become an asset to me as I work with clients. I'm able to sense and experience their emotions in our sessions, and that sense allows me to speak more deeply into their experiences.

As Christians and as the church, we should have a spiritual sixth sense—a heightened awareness for those who are struggling with their mental, emotional, physical, and spiritual health. This sixth sense is a direct result of communion, conversation, and relationship with the Holy Spirit. It must be fostered both personally and collaboratively, and it should be engaged in the same manner. I mentioned in previous chapters that caring for others well requires detailed attention to our own health and a reliance on the Holy Spirit to guide and direct. The church was built to ensure these things were acted on in such a way that the greater community is cared for.

I have the privilege of speaking often to church leadership and volunteer teams, and I always mention that the church was originally tasked with caring for the mental and emotional health of its people. If the church were empowered to engage in healing and life-giving relationships, I'd be out of a job. To be completely honest, I'd be okay with that! I know that this won't happen fully because many people don't initially turn to the church for support; however, it's interesting to think about. *What if the church, the body of Christ, were the solution to the loneliness epidemic? What if all we needed to do were readjust how we see people and how we do ministry?*

These questions remind me of Matthew 25:34-45:

[Jesus said,] "Then the King will say to those on his right, 'Enter, you who are blessed by my Father! Take what's coming to you in this kingdom. It's been ready for you since the world's foundation. And here's why:

I was hungry and you fed me,
I was thirsty and you gave me a drink,
I was homeless and you gave me a room,
I was shivering and you gave me clothes,
I was sick and you stopped to visit,
I was in prison and you came to me.'

"Then those 'sheep' are going to say, 'Master, what are you talking about? When did we ever see you hungry and feed you, thirsty and give you a drink? And when did we ever see you sick or in prison and come to you?' Then the King will say, 'I'm telling the solemn truth: Whenever you did one of these things to someone overlooked or ignored, that was me—you did it to me.'

"Then he will turn to the 'goats,' the ones on his left, and say, 'Get out, worthless goats! You're good for nothing but the fires of hell. And why? Because—

I was hungry and you gave me no meal,
I was thirsty and you gave me no drink,
I was homeless and you gave me no bed,
I was shivering and you gave me no clothes,
Sick and in prison, and you never visited.'

"Then those 'goats' are going to say, 'Master, what are you talking about? When did we ever see you hungry or thirsty or homeless or shivering or sick or in prison and didn't help?'

"He will answer them, 'I'm telling the solemn truth: Whenever you failed to do one of these things to someone who was being overlooked or ignored, that was me—you failed to do it to me.'"

This passage intrigued and disturbed me as a young Christian. I remember thinking, when I was in my late teens and early twenties, that I was going to make sure that I was a sheep, not a goat. What I didn't realize at the time is this is 100 percent due to relationship, not works. As a church, and the body of Christ, we have both an individual and a corporate responsibility to develop and grow in our relationship with God, then put relationship into action.

Jewish Justice: The Mandate to Love Others

In order to fully understand this concept of caring for "someone overlooked or ignored" (which, by the way, includes each one of us at some point in our journey), we need to understand Jewish justice. To do this, I interviewed one of my closest friends, Dr. Ryan Burkhart. Ryan and I have known each other since 2012. We work closely together at Colorado Christian University in the Clinical

Mental Health Counseling MA program, and we also get to influence the counseling field through various leadership roles, both locally and nationally. One of the things I profoundly appreciate about Ryan is his love of people and the Scriptures. Here is my interview with Ryan on the topic of Jewish justice and how it relates to the church's mandate to help eradicate the loneliness epidemic.[2]

MARK: *When you talk about the biblical concept of justice and righteousness, what do you mean?*

RYAN: Throughout the Old Testament, justice and righteousness seem inseparable. In fact, rather than being two separate ideas, they are often presented as having a codependent relationship. You can't be righteous without being just, nor can you be just without being righteous.

These co-occurring concepts are foundational pillars in living a life aligned with God's intention for humankind. For example, in 1 Kings, the queen of Sheba, after hearing of King Solomon's greatness, decides to fact-check these rumors and travels to Jerusalem to "test him with hard questions" (1 Kings 10:1, ESV). This pagan queen was amazed at King Solomon's wisdom, and proclaims that God, out of his love for Israel, made Solomon king so that he "may execute justice and righteousness" (1 Kings 10:9, ESV).

In Hosea, speaking of a betrothal covenant that it is to come, God says that he "will betroth you to me in righteousness and justice, in steadfast love and in mercy" (Hosea 2:19, ESV).

Strung throughout the *Nevi'im*, or the prophet canon of the Old Testament, are shadows of One who is to come. Much like the protoevangelium in Genesis 3:15, we see written glimpses of a King, a Savior, of One who will crush the head of evil in righteousness and justice. Jeremiah wrote, "Behold, the days are coming, declares the LORD, when I will raise up for David a righteous Branch, and he shall reign as king and deal wisely, and shall execute justice and righteousness in the land" (Jeremiah 23:5, ESV). Ten chapters later, Jeremiah again wrote, "I will cause a righteous Branch to spring up for David, and he shall execute justice and righteousness in the land" (Jeremiah 33:15, ESV).

The beauty of the Old Testament is God seems disinterested in proving himself but consumed with knowing and being known by his creation. It's as if his existence is simply a given rather than something needing to be proved. Consistently, God lets his people in on his plan, his intentions, and his hopes for his creation. These glimpses of what is to come help us see the direction he intends to take humankind. And this direction is progressively lateral rather than vertical.

Proverbs 21:3 announces, "To do righteousness and justice is more acceptable to the LORD than sacrifice" (ESV). Ultimately, it seems as though God's greatest intention for humankind is not one of temple-based worship but of being an extension of his attitude, posture, and intention within and among his creation.

MARK: *In what way does this play out in our engagement with others in their loneliness?*

RYAN: While it's immensely important to him, our God isn't solely concerned with maintaining our relationship with him. In fact, he seems as concerned with our maintaining our relationship with others. And it is within this relationship the *imago Dei* is most evident. We see this on full display with the biblical concepts of righteousness and justice.

As mentioned above, these two terms are blanketed across the Old Testament. But their consistent pairing is worth our attention.

Often, they are right next to each other, spoken within the same breath, as if the Scriptures are forcing their coupling within our minds.

The Hebrew word for righteousness is *tsedaqah*. We often understand righteousness as simply doing right by God or doing what God has commanded us to do. While this is absolutely correct, as with many words in Hebrew, this word is more than it seems at first glance. Righteousness is also associated with a concern with those around us. More specifically, it includes acts spurred on by a desire to help those in our midst reach their fullest potential, ultimately becoming self-sufficient.

In other words, being righteous involves genuine care of and empowering action for those around us. If one seeks to do right by God, they must do right by the people God has placed in their life. Righteousness exists within the dynamic of "others" in our life.

Mishpat, the Hebrew word for justice, carries similar connotations. As with *tsedaqah*, *mishpat* is more than meets the eye. The word for lawyer, *mishpatan*, comes from this Hebrew word and often captures our initial understanding. Justice is often associated with punishment or a balanced ending. While this is correct, it fails to capture the essence of this word.

The crucifixion of Jesus is ultimately captured by the concept of *mishpat*. Justice, in the Bible, is strongly concerned with equity. It deals with treating people fairly, giving them what they are due as created beings of the Most High God. This includes not only punishment but is balanced with protection and care as well. In Scripture, an unbalanced propensity toward punishment is always met with calls for just mercy. As we know too well in our culture, balanced justice is difficult to achieve outside of God.

In the greatest act of compassion our world has ever seen, our

God not only became man through Jesus Christ but also became the living definition of justice. He received our just punishment while showing mercy. The justice of Jesus led him to not see us for who we are and what we do; instead, he saw us as sons and daughters of the Holy One and treated us accordingly. What we do deserves punishment without mercy, but what we are—children of God—deserves justice.

"But let him who boasts boast in this, that he understands and knows me, that I am the LORD who practices steadfast love, justice, and righteousness in the earth. For in these things I delight, declares the LORD" (Jeremiah 9:24, ESV).

MARK: *What implications does this have for the church?*

RYAN: Together, *tsedaqah* and *mishpat* capture the messianic concept of justice. This concept has profound social implications.

To be righteous and do justice is to see those around us not for their actions but for their createdness. It is to give of oneself to help others reach their fullest potential as a son or daughter of the living God: "By him all things were created, in heaven and on earth, visible and invisible, whether thrones or dominions or rulers or authorities—all things were created through him and for him" (Colossians 1:16, ESV).

This, of course, does not mean the actions of others don't matter. Evil exists in this world, and far too often, you and I spread evil without remorse. Nor does this mean we aren't held accountable to the standards God has promulgated in his written Word to us.

But it does mean for us, individually, that our own relationship with God doesn't exist apart from our relationship with the world around us.

This is evident in Scripture's quartet of the vulnerable.[3] The poor, travelers or immigrants, widows, and orphans are consistently identified as the most vulnerable populations in biblical times. Those with minimal economic resources rarely have the means needed to reach their fullest potential. Immigrants, being away from home, were away from the support of their family systems. Widows lost their provider and protector with the passing of their husband. Orphans were left to navigate the world without the loving guidance and care of their parents.

Inevitably, God calls his people to take care of the most vulnerable around us. You can't read the book of Jeremiah, for example, without seeing God's complete frustration with his people failing to take care of those around them.

> Thus says the LORD: Do justice and righteousness, and deliver from the hand of the oppressor him who has been robbed. And do no wrong or violence to the resident alien, the fatherless, and the widow, nor shed innocent blood in this place. For if you will indeed obey this word, then there shall enter the gates of this house kings who sit on the throne of David, riding in chariots and on horses, they and their servants and their people. But if you will not obey these words, I swear by myself, declares the LORD, that this house shall become a desolation.
>
> JEREMIAH 22:3-5, ESV

Do justice and righteousness to the one who "has been robbed" and is now poor, do right by immigrants, orphans, and widows. Here, in this verse alone, Jeremiah captures the quartet of the vulnerable.

As followers of God, we must be concerned with the most vulnerable in our midst.

To be righteous, to enact justice, is to give hope to those who have lost their hope and are lonely. To those whose hope has been taken from them, at times violently. To those who have lost their hope as a result of this rocky, winding road we call life.

Church, you are called to give hope. You are called to love those around you, to empower them to be the best "them" they can be. You are righteous and just in this. This should be the natural manifestation of your relationship with God. Your lateral relationships, the relationships with those around you on earth, matter immensely to the One you are in a vertical relationship with, the one true God.

Lateral misalignment (lack of healthy boundaries) results in vertical misalignment. Vertical alignment should result in lateral alignment. In all things, your relationship with God is your foundation. This is most evident in your support and care for the hopeless around you. . . .

We have hope to offer as the *imago Dei*. This hope must be lent wisely and in life-giving ways (Colossians 4:5-6). But we can't do so until we recognize the act of giving hope as a righteous act of justice. Authentic and genuine relationships are fertile soil for seeds of hope.

Seek out those in your community who have little hope, those who are vulnerable, and show them the righteous care and just equity of Christ. Give of yourself through healthy relationship and walk beside them. Choose to be part of their story.

As a professional counselor and a counselor educator, I often teach on what makes clinical mental health services effective. Research has consistently shown the single greatest factor in clinical change to be the therapeutic relationship. It's the relationship counselors establish with their clients that causes change. In essence, counselors are professional builders of healthy relationships. Such a calling directly aligns with the restorative mission of Christ on Earth.

Early Christians called themselves *followers of the Way*. If you call yourself a Christian, you are called to the way of Christ. Your calling is one of righteousness and justice. Your calling is to bring hope to the hopeless through authentic relationship and selfless acts of just compassion, helping those around you achieve true equity by reaching their fullest potential.

Our vertical relationship demands this of us.

Be bringers of hope.

Communities of Faith

I know that loneliness won't be completely eradicated until we're reunited with Christ. The chasm of loneliness can only be filled when Christ returns. Yet I strongly believe the church is positioned to engage in this redemptive work now. We can enter the trenches with "someone overlooked or ignored" by doing six things. This isn't an exhaustive list; however, these are six key components every faith community can start with, then grow from there.

1. *Understand that need exists on a hierarchy:* Maslow's hierarchy of needs is a motivational theory used in counseling and psychology. It depicts a five-tier model of human need that can properly orient the church in how to care for people. (See Figure 7.) Maslow posited that people must have their physiological needs (food, water, warmth, rest) met first. Once those needs are met, then their safety

needs can be met. Maslow called these needs the basic needs of every human. From there, he discussed the belongingness and love needs and the esteem needs (being seen, valued, loved; and having a purpose and direction). Finally, at the top of the pyramid, Maslow described self-actualization (the ability to achieve one's fullest potential). I see this final stage of the pyramid as self-realization or self-awareness in relation to God. Maslow's pyramid gives us a practical framework for care. We must care for someone's physical needs first, then we can care for their mental, emotional, and spiritual needs.

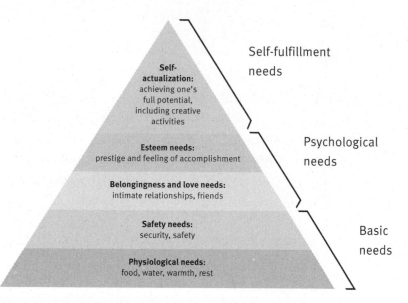

2. *Create opportunities for depth:* How are you creating opportunities for depth, as an individual and in your larger community? I go to a large church in Colorado Springs.

In years past, this church has been accused (by people on the outside) of being an out-of-touch megachurch. For those of us who actively attend, however, this couldn't be further from the truth. Why? Because the church provides countless opportunities for people to engage in depth. It has section communities, each with an assigned pastor and volunteer leaders. Each section community meets monthly for a meal and empowers its members to engage in community outside of church. It has small groups, meal groups, and Alpha groups. Essentially, this megachurch has created thousands of smaller churches within its walls to provide chances for people to engage in depth. It is up to the individual to then facilitate that depth by moving past the typical "How's the weather?" conversations to conversations that engage the soul.

3. *Model vulnerability:* Nothing is more powerful than someone leading by example. Vulnerability—the quality or state of being exposed—only catches on after it's demonstrated. It can be a scary posture to adopt—as it can leave us open for attack emotionally, mentally, and spiritually—but it can also open us up for greater connection, attachment, and healing. An example of vulnerability can be found in the attachment concept of *rupture and repair.* When we react out of selfishness or emotion, there's the possibility for damage to happen to the relationship (rupture). For example, when I react poorly to one of my daughters, I create a rupture. If I don't do anything to repair that rupture, it has the potential to grow and further the divide. If I choose to be vulnerable, however,

I can repair that rupture. In this situation, a repair would look like me getting down on my daughter's level, owning my behavior, and asking for her forgiveness. When the vulnerable repair happens, the attachment bond becomes stronger than it was before the rupture. Vulnerability has the power to heal.

4. *Allow for belonging:* In Part I of this book, I discussed the rise of tribalism as a result of people's deep desire to belong to something bigger than them. The problem is that to join a tribe, you must give up the right to question or think. For some reason, we want people to behave correctly first, then they can belong. What if this were reversed? *What if people had the opportunity to belong first, ask questions, wrestle with concepts of truth, then believe, then behave?* If this were the church's paradigm, it'd provide a judgment-free invitation to the lonely to come and figure out relationship together. It would require intentionality on behalf of the leadership and complete awareness of the messiness that would ensue. But it'd be beautiful.

5. *Make room for storytelling:* It's important for people's stories to be heard, and the church is uniquely positioned for this to happen. As a counselor, I've found that there's power in allowing people to tell their story. I often utilize the technique of narrative therapy to help people tell their story. I first have them write out their past story, detailing their experiences (good, bad, and ugly) and how they perceived those experiences. Then, I have them write about their present life experiences, and finally, I have

them write about what they want their future to look like. To help us process what was written, I have the client read their entire story to me, followed by me reading it back to them. There is power in telling a story three different ways (writing it, reading it, hearing it).

6. *Create mental and emotional health ministries:* I've had the honor of serving on a task force developed by the Department of Health and Human Services in Washington, DC, as a subset of The Partnership for Faith and Mental Health established by President George W. Bush in the early 2000s. The task force was created to develop a framework for faith groups to implement mental- and emotional-health strategies to support their congregations.[4] We found that many individuals in crisis will turn to a place of faith, prior to seeking out a mental health professional. Yet places of worship were the least equipped or prepared to work with someone with a mental- or emotional-health struggle. I believe church leadership and volunteers should be trained in mental- and emotional-health issues. This will prepare churches to minister more effectively, reduce stigma surrounding mental and emotional illness, and engage in eradicating loneliness.

These six ideas only scratch the surface of what the church can do to help people feel seen, valued, and loved. The church has the primary responsibility to be a catalyst for redemption. The church must remind people Whose they are, Whose image they were created in, Who has been pursuing them since before they were born, and Who wants to have a relationship with them. Then the church must model this in action as best as an imperfect church can, by creating opportunities for people's loneliness to be met with authentic love and compassion.

Questions for Reflection

1. How would you rate or describe your spiritual awareness?

2. What are your thoughts on the concept of Jewish justice?

3. How would you describe your current faith community? How well are they able to implement the six ideas? What could they be better at?

4. What could you do to personally enhance your faith community's response to "someone overlooked or ignored"?

THE MESSY EMBRACE
Understanding Vulnerability, Community, and Redemption

*What should young people do with their lives today? Many things, obviously.
But the most daring thing is to create stable communities in which
the terrible disease of loneliness can be cured.*

KURT VONNEGUT

*By rights, we shouldn't even be here. But we are. It's like in the great stories,
Mr. Frodo. The ones that really mattered. Full of darkness and danger, they were.
And sometimes you didn't want to know the end because how could the end be
happy? How could the world go back to the way it was when so much bad had
happened? . . . But in the end, it's only a passing thing, a shadow. Even darkness
must pass. A new day will come. And when the sun shines, it will shine out the
clearer. Those were the stories that stayed with you, that meant something. Even if
you were too small to understand why. But I think, Mr. Frodo, I do understand.
I know now. Folk in those stories had lots of chances of turning back, only they
didn't. They kept going. Because they were holding on to something.*

SAMWISE "SAM" GAMGEE, *The Two Towers*

YOU AND I are in an epic story. A story of good versus evil, a
story of love and sacrifice, a story of joy and sadness, and a story
of redemption and freedom. The perfection of relationship, connection, and fellowship was seemingly lost so long ago, yet we
have been pursued by a God who desperately wants to know us
beyond our appearance and our accomplishments. He wants to
know us at our core, intimately and passionately. The beautiful
thing is that he wants you and me to accomplish this. Almighty

God wants us. He doesn't need us in his redemptive work, but instead he *chooses to use us* in it. It's beautiful, and it's a messy collision—a messy embrace.

We must be reminded of this story because, if we aren't, we'll get lost in the nuances of the chaos.

The Vision

Several years ago, I had the honor of speaking to a group of parents who had chosen to foster and/or adopt children. My church was putting on a date night for them. They catered a dinner, provided childcare, and had me speak to them about the importance of self-care. My desire was to provide practical steps that would encourage them to find ways to implement self-care amid the busyness of their home lives.

While I was speaking, a dear friend sat in the back of the room, listening and availing himself to anyone who needed prayer during the evening. Throughout the duration of my talk, no one came up to him for prayer. When my talk concluded, he made a beeline to me and said, "Mark, while you were talking, God gave me a vision and a word of encouragement for you. May I share it with you?"

"Yes!" I replied.

"Mark, you are a loaded paintbrush. Just as an artist loads his paintbrush with color to paint a masterpiece, you, too, are a loaded paintbrush of color." He paused. "Your color is your care, love, warmth, listening ear, expertise, and presence. When people encounter you, they're changed."

He then said, "I saw a long line of people, waiting in darkness. Their presence was blackened by sin, separation, and loneliness.

They were lost and afraid. But when they embraced you, your color was transferred over to them. It didn't deplete your color in quantity or vibrancy; it simply transferred. And in that messy embrace, they were forever changed."

I stood there for a moment with tears streaming down my face. What a beautiful picture and confirmation of my calling.

As I've reflected on this word of encouragement over the years, I'm thankful for its continued affirmation of my call to care for people, but I've come to recognize this beautiful picture is not just for me—it's for all of us. This is the story of redemption. My color didn't come from me; it came from the redemptive work of Christ's sacrifice on the Cross. I, too, was darkened by my sin, my separation, and my loneliness, but I was forever changed by Christ. His color transferred to me when I embraced him, and now it's my responsibility to embrace others. This is your story too. You are a loaded paintbrush, and it's your responsibility and honor to color others' lives.

Living with Eternity in Mind

I don't know about you, but I can get caught up in the chaos of our world, the sensationalizing of the media, the divisiveness of politics, the pursuit of money, prestige, and prominence, and lose sight of what life is really about. Loneliness runs deep in our culture, and it can be cleverly disguised as mental, emotional, or physical illness. It can also be masked by the drive for success, the overuse of technology, and the rise of tribalism. The truth is we have an innate, encoded desire to be seen, known, valued, and loved, and it's our responsibility to be catalysts for this to happen for ourselves and others.

For this to unfold, we must first pursue a right relationship with God and have an appropriate love for self. Only then will we be able to confront the pervasiveness of loneliness in our world. It's important to note that when we choose to work closely with people, we forfeit the luxury of not knowing what is going on inside of us. When we're mentally, emotionally, and spiritually healthy, those around us will have a better chance of becoming emotionally healthy. We must live with eternity in mind.

One of my life verses is Isaiah 61:1-7, which clearly models what this messy embrace could look like. It says:

> The Spirit of GOD, the Master, is on me
> Because GOD anointed me.
> He sent me to preach good news to the poor,
> heal the heartbroken,
> Announce freedom to all captives,
> pardon all prisoners.
> GOD sent me to announce the year of his grace—
> a celebration of God's destruction of our enemies—
> and to comfort all who mourn,
> To care for the needs of all who mourn in Zion,
> give them bouquets of roses instead of ashes,
> Messages of joy instead of news of doom,
> a praising heart instead of a languid spirit.
> Rename them "Oaks of Righteousness"
> planted by GOD to display his glory.
> They'll rebuild the old ruins,
> raise a new city out of the wreckage.
> They'll start over on the ruined cities,
> take the rubble left behind and make it new.

THE MESSY EMBRACE

You'll hire outsiders to herd your flocks
  and foreigners to work your fields,
But you'll have the title "Priests of GOD,"
  honored as ministers of our God.
You'll feast on the bounty of nations,
  you'll bask in their glory.
Because you got a double dose of trouble
  and more than your share of contempt,
Your inheritance in the land will be doubled
  and your joy go on forever.

This Scripture passage is the fifth of Isaiah's Servant Songs.[1] Typically, a prophetic servant was anointed by the Holy Spirit to proclaim a message of deliverance to the people. (Jesus fulfilled this task of Servant when he quoted these words at the beginning of his ministry; see Luke 4:16-21.) Those of us who claim to follow Christ are therefore set apart by the anointing of the Holy Spirit to enact this very type of needed change.

According to this passage, there are several key postures that we need to adopt as we enter the loneliness of our culture.

Posture #1: Preach the Good News
This posture requires us to be truth tellers, bringing the Good News of pursuit and redemption offered by Christ. The lie of loneliness can be so pervasive that people don't realize it doesn't have to be this way. A posture of preaching the Good News means we might be revealing the truths of salvation, of entering a greater purpose and a greater community, to people who've never heard it before. We're creating a new fork in their journey by telling them that it doesn't have to be this way.

181

Posture #2: Heal the Brokenhearted

This posture requires our presence—and our ability to listen well. When was the last time you stopped to *listen*? To hear everything you needed to hear? Listening requires intentional focus, relational experience, and a keen sense of internal awareness. We hear with our ears, but we listen with our bodies. Only 10 percent of listening happens with our ears; 90 percent is what happens between the lines of speech: body language, facial cues, vocal tone, et cetera.

One of my favorite examples of listening well and healing the brokenhearted is the Jewish tradition of sitting shiva. Sitting shiva is the practice of presence, of being with people who are mourning, without attempting to fix their grief. It involves bringing food, sitting with the individuals, and laughing, crying, and sharing stories. It's intended to allow the mourning people to feel supported, loved, seen, and valued.

It takes one-hundredth of a second to pick up on body language and facial features, and three-hundredths of a second to judge or perceive what was displayed.[2] Loving by listening means that you must:

- be attentive to the one who's speaking by making eye contact and observing body language;
- be present to the entirety of the conversation;
- keep an open mind about what's being said, without jumping to conclusions;
- not interrupt or offer solutions;
- wait for the one who's speaking to finish, then share what you heard;
- ask clarifying questions; and
- seek to understand instead of trying to be right.

Listen more. Speak less. Love well.

Posture #3: Proclaim Truth

Proclaiming something means officially and clearly calling out or stating something in public. Proclaiming freedom means naming truths that exist but may be obscured by the distractions and lies of this world. It's making a public stance or statement, a declaration.

Posture #4: Rescue Those in Danger

Sometimes a posture requires deliberate action. Rescuing someone from danger requires action. We could be in an intercessory role as we speak on behalf of a lonely individual, helping them find words to make sense of their experiences. It requires us to enter their messiness and pull them out of their loneliness.

Posture #5: Comfort Those Who Mourn

This posture requires the ability to be with people without an agenda. Remember: Our presence has power, and so do our words. Our presence has the power to heal or to hurt mentally, emotionally, physically, and spiritually. So it's important for us to be okay with just *being*.

Posture #6: Plant Those Who Are Redeemed

The analogy of planting is beautiful. When you plant something, you give it new life and a new purpose. It can transform into something stronger. Here, we're taking people who have been called out, rescued, and restored and replanting them next to water so they can become firmly rooted oaks of righteousness reflecting God's glory.

* * *

When we intentionally adopt these postures, the results flow out of our obedience, not our works, as we become a conduit for the Holy Spirit to do his work. To offer an example of what this looks like, let me tell you about my friend Matthew. Over a decade ago, Matthew and his family went through a major ordeal. His daughter had chosen to engage in a different lifestyle, and her choices took her down a path that wasn't ideal. Matthew and his wife stayed consistent in their prayers for her, and their daughter eventually came back around.

One day, she asked her dad to drive her to a doctor's appointment because she needed a physical for a new job. "Mark," Matthew stated as he told me this story, "when she got back into the car, I realized this had nothing to do with a physical, but that she was pregnant." He paused. "As I was sitting in that moment, I had to take a deep breath. I looked at her and asked, 'This wasn't a physical, was it?' With tears streaming down her face, she revealed that she was pregnant.

"Mark, I paused for what seemed like an eternity, and in that time, I heard the Holy Spirit whisper, *How you handle this situation will determine your relationship with her for the rest of your life*. With tears in my eyes, I reached over to hug her and told her I loved her and that we'd figure it out."

What a perfect, beautiful picture of a messy embrace. It wasn't easy for Matthew to respond in that way because he was saddened and upset. But his daughter needed to be seen, loved, valued, and heard. She needed to be told and shown that she wasn't alone. The results were messy, but the relationship was intact.

In the same way, when we deliberately model the six postures outlined above, these results will follow:

- truth will be heard;
- hearts will be made whole;
- chains will be loosed;
- captives will be rescued;
- beauty will be revealed, and heaviness will be lifted; and
- lonely people we embrace will be given a second chance.

We live in a world full of uncertainty. This statement is more evident now than ever. Mental, emotional, physical, and spiritual distress is running rampant in our communities—and is directly linked to this loneliness epidemic. Solutions will seem elusive if we follow any of the many rabbit trails in front of us. But if we choose to take a step back and see the bigger picture, the solution becomes clear. We must find ways to lean into, be present with, engage in, and heal our own inner narratives so we can be present for others in their struggles.

It's a messy embrace we make as we journey with people toward healing, toward Christ, and toward wholeness. Everyone's healing will look different, and everyone's healing will be messy as individuals sort out their emotions, hurts, frustrations, and uncertainties with your loving, encouraging presence.

Yes, it's true that we never fully arrive this side of heaven, but we must be intentional about maintaining the course. Persistent loneliness has a greater chance of dying in relational community. We must have patience with each other, and we must couple it with persistence and grace.

Acknowledgments

Sarah Mayfield, thank you for allowing me to pursue my dreams. Thank you for your constant love and encouragement.

Hannah and Elle, I love being your daddy! I hope this book creates a better world for you to live in.

Dad and Mom, thank you for raising me to care for and love others. Your example made me who I am today.

Joni Jones, thank you for listening to my crazy ideas, having wonderful conversations about mental and emotional health, and being an amazing mother-in-law.

Dr. Ryan Burkhart, you are an amazing friend! I am honored to collaborate with you on so many amazing projects. Thanks for being such a good friend.

Greg Johnson, thank you for encouraging me over a decade ago to let my story gain experience.

Ashley Wiersma, thank you for believing in me and connecting me to Robert Wolgemuth.

Don Pape, thank you for taking a chance on me and allowing me to write this book!

Robert Wolgemuth, thank you for helping me bring this book to life!

Notes

INTRODUCTION

1. *WALL-E*, directed by Andrew Stanton (Burbank, CA: Walt Disney Studios Home Entertainment, 2008).
2. Georgina Fuller, "Young & Lonely," *Community Practitioner* 92, no. 2 (2019): 40–43.
3. Postvention is an organized response after a tragedy, such as a suicide. It is a collaborative effort by like-minded organizations to help the community heal.

CHAPTER 1: LONELINESS

1. Christian Jarrett, "Why Meeting Another's Gaze Is So Powerful," bbc.com, January 8, 2019, https://www.bbc.com/future/article/20190108-why -meeting-anothers-gaze-is-so-powerful#:~:text=They%20concluded %20that%2C%20on%20average,lasted%20longer%20than%20nine %20seconds).&text=Another%20documented%20effect%20of%20mutual ,can%20sometimes%20feel%20so%20compelling.
2. Here and throughout, unless otherwise noted, names and identifying details have been changed to protect individuals' identities.
3. *Merriam-Webster's Collegiate Dictionary*, 10th ed. (1993), s.v. "lonely."
4. "2018 Cigna U.S. Loneliness Index," Cigna, accessed March 2, 2021, https://www.cigna.com/static/www-cigna-com/docs/about-us/newsroom /studies-and-reports/combatting-loneliness/loneliness-survey-2018-full -report.pdf.

5. Minor edits were made to these and following survey responses to enhance readability (meaning was maintained).

CHAPTER 2: THE PERSONAL COST OF LONELINESS

1. Jean M. Twenge, *iGen: Why Today's Super-Connected Kids Are Growing Up Less Rebellious, More Tolerant, Less Happy—and Completely Unprepared for Adulthood—and What That Means for the Rest of Us* (New York: Atria Paperback, 2017), 102.

2. Twenge, *iGen*, 103–104.

3. "Facts & Statistics," Anxiety and Depression Association of America, accessed January 19, 2021, https://adaa.org/about-adaa/press-room /facts-statistics.

4. "Depression," Anxiety and Depression Association of America, accessed January 19, 2021, https://adaa.org/understanding-anxiety/depression.

5. "Anxiety and Depression in Children," Anxiety and Depression Association of America, accessed March 2, 2021, https://adaa.org/find-help/by -demographics/children/anxiety-and-depression.

6. National Institute of Mental Health, "Suicide," accessed January 19, 2021, https://www.nimh.nih.gov/health/statistics/suicide.shtml#:~:text =During%20that%2020%2Dyear%20period,females%20(6.2%20per %20100%2C000).

7. "Suicide Facts," Suicide Awareness Voices of Education (SAVE), accessed March 8, 2021, https://save.org/about-suicide/suicide-facts/.

8. *Oxford Online Dictionary*, s.v. "emotional intelligence, (*n*.)," accessed January 13, 2021, https://www.lexico.com/en/definition/emotional _intelligence.

9. Betty Rintoul et al., *Factors in Child Development, Part I: Personal Characteristics and Parental Behavior*, August 1998, http://www.rti.org /sites/default/files/resources/child-development.pdf.

10. "Does Heart Disease Run in Your Family?" CDC, last reviewed February 3, 2021, https://www.cdc.gov/genomics/disease/heart_disease .htm#:~:text=Each%20year%20in%20the%20United,likely%20to %20develop%20heart%20disease.

11. "Cancer Facts & Figures 2020," American Cancer Society, accessed March 8, 2021, https://www.cancer.org/research/cancer-facts-statistics /all-cancer-facts-figures/cancer-facts-figures-2020.html#:~:text=The %20Facts%20%26%20Figures%20annual%20report,deaths%20in %20the%20United%20States.

12. Stephanie Brooks Holliday and Wendy M. Troxel, "Relationship Quality: Implications for Sleep Quality and Sleep Disorders," in *Family Contexts*

of Sleep and Health Across the Life Course, eds. Susan M. McHale, Valarie King, and Orfeu M. Buxton (Cham, Switzerland: Springer, 2017), 53–84.

13. Thomas Cowan, *Human Heart, Cosmic Heart: A Doctor's Quest to Understand, Treat, and Prevent Cardiovascular Disease* (White River Junction, VT: Chelsea Green, 2016), 8–9.

14. Cowan, *Human Heart*, 9–10.

15. From Stephanie Seneff et al., "A Novel Hypothesis for Atherosclerosis as a Cholesterol Sulfate Deficiency Syndrome," *Theoretical Biology and Medical Modelling* 12, no. 1 (2015).

16. Cowan, *Human Heart*, 15.

17. Somayeh Ramesh, Mohammad Ali Besharat, and Hossein Nough, "Relationship between Worry, and Anger Rumination with Cardiovascular Disease Severity: Social Loneliness as a Moderator," *Archives of Iranian Medicine (AIM)* 23, no. 3 (March 2020): 175–180.

18. David B. Feldman and Jonathan R. Sills, "Hope and Cardiovascular Health-Promoting Behaviors: Education Alone Is Not Enough," *Psychology & Health* 28, no. 7 (2013): 727–45.

19. Bina Nausheen et al., "Loneliness, Social Support and Cardiovascular Reactivity to Laboratory Stress," *Stress* 10, no. 1 (2007): 37–44.

20. Louise C. Hawkley and John T. Cacioppo, "Loneliness and Pathways to Disease," *Brain, Behavior, and Immunity* 17, no. 1 (2003): 98–105.

CHAPTER 3: THE CULTURAL CONUNDRUM

1. "Survey: The Average Household Owns 7 Screens," PR Newswire, May 25, 2017, https://www.prnewswire.com/news-releases/survey-the -average-household-owns-7-screens-300464065.html.

2. You and Your Hormones, "Melatonin," reviewed March 2018, https:// www.yourhormones.info/hormones/melatonin/.

3. Jennifer F. Cross, "What Does Too Much Screen Time Do to Children's Brains?" NewYork-Presbyterian, accessed January 21, 2021, https:// healthmatters.nyp.org/what-does-too-much-screen-time-do-to-childrens -brains/. The referenced study is the Adolescent Brain Cognitive Development Study, which is ongoing; learn more at www.abcdstudy.org.

4. See Chuck Hadad, "Why Some 13-Year-Olds Check Social Media 100 Times a Day," updated October 13, 2015, https://www.cnn.com/2015 /10/05/health/being-13-teens-social-media-study/index.html.

5. I would challenge you to watch the documentary *#Being13*. You can find it on YouTube.

6. "In a World That's Always On, We Are Trapped in the 'Present,'" interview with Douglas Rushkoff, March 25, 2013, All Things Considered (NPR),

https://www.npr.org/2013/03/25/175056313/in-a-world-thats-always-on
-we-are-trapped-in-the-present#:~:text=%22%20'Digiphrenia'%20is
%20really%20the,yourself%20at%20the%20same%20time. See also
Rushkoff's book, *Present Shock: When Everything Happens Now* (New York:
Current, 2014), 75.

7. George Packer, "A New Report Offers Insight into Tribalism in the Age
   of Trump," *The New Yorker*, October 13, 2018, http://www.newyorker
   .com/news/daily-comment/a-new-report-offers-insights-into-tribalism
   -in-the-age-of-trump.

8. Packer, "A New Report."

CHAPTER 5: IT WAS MEANT TO BE THIS WAY

1. "Suzana Herculano-Houzel: Neuroscientist," ted.com, accessed March 1,
   2021, https://www.ted.com/speakers/suzana_herculano_houzel.

2. Stanford University Medical Center, "Stunning Details of Brain
   Connections Revealed," ScienceDaily, November 17, 2010, https://
   www.sciencedaily.com/releases/2010/11/101117121803.htm.

3. Paul Reber, "What Is the Memory Capacity of the Human Brain?"
   Scientific American, May 1, 2010, https://www.scientificamerican.com
   /article/what-is-the-memory-capacity/#:~:text=You%20might%20have
   %20only%20a,(or%20a%20million%20gigabytes).

4. "72 Amazing Human Brain Facts (Based on the Latest Science)," San
   Diego Brain Injury Foundation, February 22, 2019, https://sdbif.org
   /index/72-amazing-human-brain-facts-based-on-the-latest-science
   /#:~:text=A%20piece%20of%20brain%20tissue,all%20communicating
   %20with%20each%20other.

5. Guinness World Records, "Fastest Speed Outright in a Formula One
   Grand Prix," accessed March 2, 2021, https://www.guinnessworldrecords
   .com/world-records/fastest-speed-outright-in-a-formula-one-grand-prix.

6. "72 Amazing Human Brain Facts (Based on the Latest Science)," San
   Diego Brain Injury Foundation, February 22, 2019, https://sdbif.org
   /index/72-amazing-human-brain-facts-based-on-the-latest-science
   /#:~:text=Your%20brain%20generates%20about%2012,blood%20flows
   %20through%20the%20brain.

7. Anne Trafton, "Neuroscientists Reveal How the Brain Can Enhance
   Connections," MIT News, November 19, 2015, http://news.mit.edu
   /2015/brain-strengthen-connections-between-neurons-1118.

8. Chad Luke, *Neuroscience for Counselors and Therapists: Integrating the Science
   of the Mind and Brain*, 2nd ed. (San Diego: Cognella, 2020), 37–49.

9. Daniel J. Siegel and Mary Hartzell, *Parenting from the Inside Out: How*

a Deeper Self-Understanding Can Help You Raise Children Who Thrive
(New York: Jeremy P. Tarcher/Penguin, 2014), 90. Our understanding
of how the brain works is constantly growing.

CHAPTER 6: THE DEEP LONGING

1. Inside Out, directed by Pete Docter and Ronnie Del Carmen
   (Emeryville, CA: Pixar, 2015).
2. Daniel J. Siegel, *Brainstorm: The Power and Purpose of the Teenage Brain*
   (New York: Jeremy P. Tarcher/Penguin, 2015), 150–151.
3. Imants Baruss, "Quantum Theories of Consciousness," *Baltic Journal
   of Psychology* 7, no. 1 (2006): 39–45; Zamzuri Idris, "Quantum
   Physics Perspective on Electromagnetic and Quantum Fields Inside the
   Brain," *Maylays J Med Sci.* 27, no. 1 (February 2020): 1–5; and Syed
   Ismyl Mahmood Rizvi, "Quantum Mechanics of 'Conscious Energy,'"
   International Journal of Mind, Brain & Cognition 9, nos. 1–2 (2018):
   132–160.
4. "Waves and Wavelengths," Lumen, accessed January 13, 2021, http://
   courses.lumenlearning.com/wsu-sandbox/chapters/waves-and-wavelengths.

CHAPTER 7: MODEL FOR ACTION

1. Bible Hub, "2588. kardia," accessed March 2, 2021, https://biblehub
   .com/greek/2588.htm.

CHAPTER 8: INDIVIDUAL RESPONSIBILITY

1. John Bunyan, *The Pilgrim's Progress: From This World to That Which Is to
   Come*, accessed January 29, 2021, https://www.gutenberg.org/files/131
   /131-h/131-h.htm.
2. Henri Nouwen with Michael J. Christensen and Rebecca J. Laird, *Spiritual
   Direction: Wisdom for the Long Walk of Faith* (New York: HarperOne,
   2015), 28–30.
3. Henri Nouwen, *The Way of the Heart: Desert Spirituality and Contemporary
   Ministry* (San Francisco: HarperSanFrancisco, 1991), 30, 32.

CHAPTER 9: PERSONAL RESPONSIBILITY

1. Kendra Cherry, "The 6 Stages of Behavior Change: The Transtheoretical
   or Stages of Change Model," Verywell Mind, updated November 19,
   2020, https://www.verywellmind.com/the-stages-of-change-2794868.
   The termination phase can also be the relapse phase for some, meaning
   they start the process all over again. It is always the goal to get to the
   termination phase without relapse.

THE PATH OUT OF LONELINESS

2. J. R. R. Tolkien, *The Lord of the Rings*, one volume, 50th anniversary ed. (Boston: Houghton Mifflin, 2012), 940.

CHAPTER 10: FAITH COMMUNITIES
1. "What Is a Highly Sensitive Person? (A Relatable Guide)," Highly Sensitive Refuge, accessed March 2, 2021, https://highlysensitiverefuge .com/what-is-highly-sensitive-person/. Note that some people with this trait are highly sensitive in two or three of these areas (physical, mental, emotional).
2. Shared with permission.
3. This phrase was coined by Nicholas Wolterstorff in *Justice: Rights and Wrongs* (Princeton, NJ: Princeton University Press, 2008), chap. 3.
4. For further information, go to https://www.hhs.gov/sites/default/files /compassion-in-action.pdf.

CHAPTER 11: THE MESSY EMBRACE
1. David Jeremiah, *The Jeremiah Study Bible: NKJV* (Franklin, TN: Worthy, 2013), 951.
2. Emotion psychologist Dr. Paul Eckman's contribution to the science of interpreting facial expressions is unparalleled. To learn more about his work, visit https://www.paulekman.com.

About the Author

DR. MARK MAYFIELD is a licensed professional counselor (LPC), a board-certified counselor, and the founder and CEO of Mayfield Counseling Centers.

He has more than fourteen years of professional counseling experience in clinical, judicial, and faith-based counseling settings across a wide range of patient demographics. Mayfield has professional experience in treating and addressing anxiety, depression, PTSD, substance abuse, domestic violence, self-injury, and suicide.

In addition to *The Path out of Loneliness*, he is the author of *Help! My Teen Is Self-Injuring: A Crisis Manual for Parents*. He has been featured in prominent media outlets, including *Woman's Day*, HelloGiggles, NBC, *Reader's Digest*, and Byrdie. Dr. Mayfield was invited to the White House in December of 2019 with a group of mental health professionals and has had periodic calls with the White House to discuss mental health in America.

For more about Mark, visit www.drmayfield.com. Find practical mental health resources at www.mayfieldcollective.com. Connect with Mark on Facebook and Instagram (@thedrmayfield).